View from the Mountain

View from the Mountain

Mountain

David J. Griffin

Jerlene Rose, Editor
Janice Lee Odom, Acquisitions Editor
April Smith, Graphic Design

....

A Read Writers Publishing Book
Clay City, Kentucky

Published by
Read Writers Publishing
A Division of Parkway Publications, LLC
All rights reserved.

Editorial and Sales Offices: Read Writers Publishing
295 Forge Mill Road, P. O. Box 710, Clay City KY 40312-0710
606-663-1011
www.readwriters.com

ISBN: 978-0-9858794-4-0
Library of Congress Control Number: 2012947304

This book is printed on acid-free recycled paper.

Printed and manufactured in the United States of America

Dedicated to
my beloved mother,
Ruby (Bee) Griffin

My wife, Katherine

Acknowledgements

I would like to thank my wife, Katherine, who helped convince me that I had the ability to tell my stories for publication. She also assisted me by editing each story in the book.

My brother Al and his wife, Eva, have been an invaluable source for details, names, and places in and around Rockcastle County. Eva alone is a genealogical expert – she knows everyone! It is astonishing. Al, of course, was able to supply forgotten details about life on our small family farm.

Bud and Shirley Cox – who have been my most loyal supporters – have provided me with ideas for stories and with details that I had failed to recall. My life-long friends have encouraged me from day one.

I could never forget to mention Marty Cox, who was one of my closest friends during my years at Mt. Vernon High School. She has continued her role as cheerleader – this time it has been "Go, Dave, go!" (instead of "Go, Red Devils, go!")

Several of my friends who were in my class at MVHS have been very supportive over the years concerning my weekly columns. They include: Charles Shivel, Sam Barnes, Mattie Petrey, Bill Croucher, Charlotte Loudermilk, Virginia Rose McBee, Sandy Murrell, Gary Coffee, Marion Whitehouse, and Sharon Burton.

Other friends who were slightly older than me also have continued to support my writing endeavors, including: Nancy O'Neal, Patsy Barnett, Robert Cummins, Gary Foster, Jimmy Lambert, Bobby Harper, Charles Hensley, Mary Ellen Rhoney, Bonnie Crowe, Michael Hunt, Faye Cummins, Oscar and Helen Fain, and Lloyd Fain. Lloyd and I put many miles on my old '58 Chevy.

A special thanks to my friends at the "Table of Knowledge" at the Stanton DQ, the staff of Powell County Schools, and my many friends of Powell, Montgomery, and Clark counties for their support and encouragement.

I would also like to thank *The Clay City Times* and *The Mt. Vernon Signal* for giving me the opportunity to tell my stories. Without them this book would not be possible.

Finally, I want to thank Jerlene Rose and Read Writers Publishing for their confidence in my "story telling" ability and for making this compilation a reality.

Sara Walter Combs
Judge, Kentucky Court of Appeals

Preface
By Sara Combs

How it began I cannot say for certain. It may have been in casual comments in reaction to a certain event: "Well, as Mommie Katie used to say, ..." Or it may have been at our kitchen table at the office after a long day when we would regale one another with, "Do you remembers?"

But little by little, Dave Griffin's journey into yesteryear, into "memory land," emerged and took form – to the delight of his avid fans and readers of *The Clay City Times* in Powell County. And then it spread all the way back home to Rockcastle County as his weekly articles created a unique readership in *The Signal*.

In his *View from the Mountain*, Dave Griffin, science teacher turned writer, has resurrected the spirits of loved ones who shaped his life. We all have images of Bee, Mommie Katie, and Pop. Did they resemble the characters in Mayberry? Possibly. But no matter. They have come back to life in our imaginations – as have our first cars, our first sweethearts, and our "firsts" of everything meaningful from our own long-agos.

Like a sorcerer with a pen instead of a wand, he has conjured them all back to life from the shallow graves of our memories. And we follow him, Pied-Piper like, back to our own memories because we simply can no longer resist. For in retrieving our past, we enrich the present – or at least make it more tolerable. And we discover a roadmap for an uncertain future – making it seem more certain – or at least more hopeful.

Perhaps we love our artists because they give us not only permission but the means to remember, to dream, to imagine. Henry Ward Beecher said it best: "Every artist dips his brush in his own soul and paints his own nature into his pictures."

View from the Mountain surely reveals the soul of Dave Griffin. But it is an invitation, a ticket, an "all aboard" to take that journey into our own souls.

It is a book to be loved.

The Old Homeplace

Pine Grove area of Rockcastle County

Cast of Characters

Mommie Katie – My maternal grandmother, Mary Katherine Stokes, who helped raise me.

Pop – My maternal grandfather, Eugene Stokes, who taught me the skills of being a man.

Bee – My mother, Ruby Stokes Griffin. Everyone referred to her as "Bee" for my entire life. In our family, she was never called Mother, Mom, or by any other name. She was just our Bee!

Daddy – My father, Hobe Griffin. He and my mother divorced when I was around six years of age.

Al – My older brother (I also have a younger brother, **Dwight**, by my father's second marriage.)

Eva – Al's wife, who has always been a sister to me.

Uncle Charlie – The husband of Bee's only sister, Ruth. He was one of my heroes.

Bud Cox – My lifelong friend, who accompanied me through most of my high school days and who remains one of my best friends to this day.

Contents

All in the Family..15

    My Grandfather, My Hero..................................17

    George Washington Special................................21

    Charlie Brown..25

    Hobe's Taxi Service 29

    Joyland Park 33

    Lightning Strikes Again.....................................37

    Mommie Katie's Apron 41

    Pop's Push Mower 45

    Mommie Katie's Pocketbook.............................49

    Small Town Southern Man................................53

    The Chicken House...57

    The Warm Morning Stove.................................61

Growing Pains..65

    My Heroes Have Always Been Cowboys 67

    Being a Child in the 50s 71

    Boyhood Slingshot..75

    Let the Night Games Begin...............................79

    Blackberry Season...83

    Knuckle Down 87

    The Transistor Radio...91

    Hi-yo, Silver, Away!..95

    A Most Unusual Tree Fort 99

    Pinball Wizard 103

    Making Shavings with Pop 107

    Halloween Carnival...111

The Teen Years 115

    Friends Helping Friends 117

Contents

Learning to Drive...121

Hub Caps and White Walls...............................125

Class Rings Become Precious Mementoes...........129

A Day at Mt. Vernon High...............................133

The Little World's Fair....................................137

Skating - On a Roll Again................................141

My Chevrolet..145

My First Pizza Pie 149

Life at Lebanon House 153

The Tale of the Watermelon Truck 157

Travelin' with Bud 161

Cruisin'... 165

Black Beauty..167

Boys and Their Cars 171

Kingsmen 175

Date Night - Summer 1960 179

Hamm's Drive-In Restaurant 185

Midnight Rendezvous......................................189

Midnight Run to Bristol 193

My '63 Super Sport was Sweet.........................197

Rock n' Roll 201

American Bandstand 203

Stereo Arrived with "Be-Bop-A-Lula" 207

Rock and Roll - The Soundtrack of My Life........211

I Like that Old Time Rock and Roll 217

The Day the Music Died..................................221

Sweet Success 225

August Football Memories 227

Silver in the Mine 231

Niece Debbie, me, Eva, Pop, Bee, and Mommie Katie

All in the Family

Eugene Stokes, "Pop"

My Grandfather, My Hero

When I was six years old, my mother and I moved in with my grandparents in Mt. Vernon, Kentucky. My grandfather's name was Eugene Stokes, and he was 63 at the time. I always called him Pop. We lived there for several years. As a result of the time that I spent with him, my grandfather became my all-time hero. He taught me all the things that a man needs to teach his son: how to fish and hunt, how to drive a car, how to build things, and, most importantly, how to treat other people.

Even though I was not eager to do chores at a young age, he was able to instill in me a strong work ethic. I have never met anyone who worked harder than my grandfather. He knew how to take care of everything on our small farm. I was always amazed at the skills he possessed. To me, he knew everything, and I loved to watch him complete his daily tasks. Each time he did something new, he made me watch and learn.

When I was about 10 years old, Pop decided that it was time for me to learn how to hunt small game. Early one Saturday morning, he told me to get dressed and come with him. He said we were going to get my first shotgun. When we arrived at the local hardware store, he asked his friend, who owned the store, to let me see a Stevens 20-gauge, single-barrel shotgun. I loved it immediately! Seeing that I was so excited, Pop made the purchase and we left.

When we returned home, he said we should go to our woods and practice using my new shotgun. It did not take long for him to instruct me properly concerning gun safety and how to use the gun.

The next morning, he actually took me with him squirrel hunting. When we entered the woods, he said, "Be very quiet and watch for leaves that are moving."

Within a mere 15 minutes we saw a squirrel on a limb, and he told me to wait for it to move into an opening in the leaves and to shoot when I could get a clear view. He moved away to let me watch by myself. Sure enough, the squirrel walked out on the limb, I fired my first shot, and it fell from the tree. As it fell, my grandfather stepped from behind the tree and caught the squirrel before it hit the ground. I was so proud. He then walked up to me and taught me a very valuable lesson. He said, "Son, we never kill anything that we are not going to eat." We continued our adventure, and he also bagged a couple of squirrels before we finally went home.

My next lesson was to learn how to clean a squirrel so that we could eat it. He was very methodical. Each animal was cleaned exactly the same way, a process that he called "barking" a squirrel. That evening my grandmother cooked our game, and we had a meal that I will never forget.

I admired Pop very much, but I don't think I ever loved my grandfather more than I did that night. In a single day, he had given me much more than a shotgun (which I still own); he had provided me with skills, principles, and values which have served me well and remain part of my life's philosophy.

The George Washington Special

The George Washington Special

The year was 1958; I was 14 years of age. My mother, Bee, and I boarded the majestic train known as the *George Washington Special* bound for Washington, D.C. We left from Lexington on a short vacation to visit my older brother and his wife, who had recently moved to Manassas, Virginia. Albert was serving as pastor of the Woodbine Baptist Church there. The *George Washington* did not unload passengers in Manassas; therefore, Al and his wife, Eva, were to meet us at Union Station in D.C., which was approximately 30 miles from their house.

At its inaugural on April 30, 1932, the *George Washington* was C&O Railroad's top-notch train. It was one of only two all air-conditioned, long-distance trains operating in America. Just before we decided to take the trip, it was completely refurbished by Pullman and by C&O. *Tracks Magazine* reported, "The newly redesigned George is a sizeable train with its engine, three baggage cars, a diner, three coaches, and four Pullman cars."

I was thrilled to take an excursion on such a special train. When we boarded, Bee and I stashed our bags, settled down, and tried to contain our excitement when we felt the engine pull out of the L & N Depot. It was late afternoon, and we watched the familiar scenery through our window as we headed east.

After a few miles, I decided to take a walk. My first stop was the diner, where I ordered some fries and a Coke. If my recollection is correct, the bill was nearly $6. When I later told Bee about the cost, she responded, "We can just wait until we get to Albert's before we eat again." However, she got hungry the next morning and ordered what I remember was a skimpy breakfast for the two of us to share.

When the black of night had obscured our view, we settled down into the comfortable seats and were lulled to sleep by the steady rhythm of the wheels on the track. After a short nap, it was difficult for me to stay in one place while on board this exciting ride. With Bee still sleeping, I quietly got up and walked to the back of the last car where you could step outside and watch as the tracks disappeared into the darkness. I stood there for a long time just feeling the sensation of the train as it rocked gently from side to side. Occasionally, I got a glimpse of the engine as we traveled around a curve.

During the night, the *George* carried us through parts of the famous Shenandoah Valley and the Blue Ridge Mountains. We also passed through the 4,263-foot Blue Ridge Tunnel, which was one of the longest tunnels in the world at that time. I could hear the moan of the whistle as we passed through small towns in West Virginia and Virginia. We only stopped at major cities along the way.

The next morning, we visited the washrooms in order to freshen up before meeting Al and Eva. We again took our seats next to the window in order to catch of view of the famous monuments in Washington. We passed by several, and both of us were thrilled to see them for the first time. The Conductor finally announced "Union Station!"

It was simply magnificent! Union Station is considered to be an historic example of the finest architecture. At that time, the Station covered more ground than any other building in the United States and was the largest train station in the world. It was a city within a city. Even today, Union Station's marble floors echo with the footsteps of over 29 million people each year, making it the most visited site in all of Washington, D.C.

We departed the train and finally met Al and Eva, who gave us a driving tour of the city before we went to their home. I could not get enough of the sights. This was my first of many visits to the city.

In 1960, I was able to ride the *George Washington* one more time. Al and Eva had visited Mt. Vernon and invited me to go home with them. After spending a few days in Manassas, I boarded the *George* to make my way home to Kentucky. The trip was completely different because I was familiar with the train. But I again found myself standing on the back of the last car watching the tracks slipping away. I was mesmerized by the sight, sound, and feel of being on a train. I am so glad that my older brother provided a reason for me to spend time on the *George Washington Special*.

Me in 8th grade

My Uncle Charlie

Charlie Brown

W hile growing up, I had my own personal "Charlie Brown." He was one of my favorite uncles and the coolest guy I knew.

Charles David Brown was the husband of my mother's sister, Ruth, and my mom had named me after him. I think because my mother and I lived with her parents, he tried to be a sort of surrogate father to me. He always paid me a lot of attention and made me feel like he actually enjoyed my company. I remember my mother telling me about him coming home from the War when I was just a baby.

Before he was drafted into the army, Uncle Charlie had attended Cumberland College and had received his teacher's certification from Eastern Kentucky University. He taught grade school in Rockcastle County. After receiving a couple of deferments, he finally decided to let the armed services proceed with drafting him. The Army made use of his teaching skills, assigning him to teach English to foreign officers in Puerto Rico and in Colombia.

Later in his life, Uncle Charles owned the Brown Monument Works on Walton Avenue in Lexington. During the summer, I occasionally got to visit my aunt and uncle, and he would let me go to work with him. It was so fascinating to watch him take a huge piece of polished marble, attach a piece of rubber to the face of the stone, and draw letters by hand on the rubber. Next, he used a razor knife to remove the letters. Then he cranked up the sand blaster, and I would watch the names on the gravestone appear as they were cut into the huge slab of marble. To a young impressionable boy, this constituted a miracle. He could actually carve names in stone!

I loved it when Aunt Ruth and Uncle Charles came to visit us in Mt. Vernon. He spent time talking to me and doing special things with me. Their daughter, Janis, was just a few years younger than I, and we played together. One day when they had come to visit, I showed her how to smoke a Catalpa Tree cigar. She got choked; I thought she was going to die. She ran into the house and told on me, and my mother almost wrung my neck. I never did that again.

Each year Uncle Charlie allowed me to go on vacations with his family–a real treat for me as my own family did not travel. It was so much fun. We usually went to the beach in Florida and stayed in a cottage. Janis and I would play in the surf and sand for hours. One year, Uncle Charlie used the opportunity to teach me how to swim. He even rented rafts for us to use to ride the waves. At night, we went to really nice restaurants, and I was always told to order whatever I wanted! He was my hero!

When I became a teenager, our talks turned more manly, revolving around Cincinnati Reds baseball or University of Kentucky sports. Uncle Charles and I would watch such sporting events on TV together, and he taught me lots of facts about the game. Again, it seemed that he was trying to be sort of a father figure to me. I don't think I ever told him how much this meant to me. His influence helped to shape my formative years. I could always ask him anything, and he would attempt to give me the most appropriate answer for a boy to hear. Any boy needs this when they are impressionable and generally curious about life.

One of the most amusing things about Uncle Charles was the fact that he was a Democrat, and the rest of the family were die-hard Republicans. He tormented my grandfather by teasing him about politics. Pop would get so mad when Uncle Charles would disparage a Republican politician. Pop was a ticket man — vote the party. Uncle Charles actually voted for the man rather than the party. Once Pop was sufficiently riled, you could see the gleam in Uncle Charles's eye. Political discussions were a joy to him.

Uncle Charles was a very bright and well read man. He even was a minister for a time. Yet (even though he exercised Christian principles), he still occasionally shared a "mature" joke with me or other members of the family. My mother particularly enjoyed this aspect of his personality. He was a significant source of laughter for her throughout her life.

Uncle Charles turned 90 in September and now lives in an apartment in Lexington. (Aunt Ruth has been gone now for several years.) "I play cards with some friends and work puzzles," he said when I asked what now occupies his time. I hope that he understands how much he influenced my life. Thank you, Uncle Charlie, for taking the time.

[Uncle Charles passed on not terribly long after this column was originally published. Both he and his daughter, Janis, were elated upon reading it, and I am so glad that he saw it before his death.]

My brother Al with Dad and friend Bobby Lay

Hobe's Taxi Service

Before I was a gleam in my father's eye, Daddy was delivering packages from the L&N Depot in Mt. Vernon. In those days, the job of delivering packages was referred to as a "dray man." (*Dray* means to haul.) It was during WWII, and Daddy delivered Western Union telegraph messages from the War Department that also arrived by way of the train depot. This gave him the horrid task of delivering messages about soldiers who had lost their lives in battle.

Since he was so consistently present at the L&N Station, lots of folks coming into Mt. Vernon on the train would ask him to take them home in his pickup truck. That gave Daddy a bright idea – a taxi service was obviously needed, and it would need to cover the entire county. At that time, the Greyhound Bus Station was located across the street from the depot in the building that later became the Dinner Bell Restaurant. His idea quickly became a reality.

Daddy started his business with a 1940 maroon Chevrolet. He had the rear windows lettered with the name, "Hobe Griffin's Taxi." It was a time in which gasoline was less than 25 cents per gallon. He figured how much it would cost him to transport individuals to specific places in the county and in nearby cities. After hand printing a list of places and the cost per person to transport them, he placed it above his visor.

Over the next few years, his business grew continuously until he finally had three taxis in his fleet. Several men in the county drove for Daddy; they included: Bobby Carter, "Piggy" Southard, Hobart Hansel, and my brother Al.

Eventually Daddy moved his taxi stand into a small room between the Ideal Café and McBee's Department Store on Main Street in Mt.Vernon. All three cabs stayed busy carrying people throughout the county.

Many individuals did not have automobiles (especially during the war), and lots of people depended upon Daddy to bring them to town for their mail, banking, grocery shopping and other essential needs.

Needless to say, it was a little strange to have a taxi as the family automobile. Each day, Daddy took me to school and then came after me in the afternoon in one of his cabs. Sometimes he even had paying passengers with him when he picked me up.

On Sunday afternoons, the family occasionally went for drives in his cab. When sitting in the rear seat, it was hard to see out because of the lettering on the windows. My brother Al learned to pronounce the letters backward (ixat sniffirg eboh) and joked about it all the time.

I also remember Daddy taking the family to the Smoky Mountains one summer in the taxi. People thought some rich family had hired a taxi to bring them to Tennessee from Kentucky. It was sort of embarrassing.

I distinctly remember a bear coming up to the side of the automobile and my brother asking Daddy if the bear wanted us to take him somewhere. Daddy did not think that was funny.

When I was very young, Daddy would occasionally allow me to go with him on his taxi runs. There was one night when I was with him that he picked up a passenger who had consumed a little too much to drink, and he paid his cab fare with a sock full of coins. Frankly, it disgusted my father [expletives deleted], and he did not even bother to count the change. Instead he gave me the sock filled with money for my piggy bank.

I guess that I have always remembered that incident because I thought that it was just too cool. I definitely recall hoping that we would pick up more men who were under the influence of alcohol.

Daddy once told us about another event that happened when he had a customer who was drinking. The man said that he needed to go to the Sand Springs area. When they were almost there, he hit

Daddy in the back of the head with a whisky bottle, jumped out, and ran into the woods. (I am certain that Daddy pulled out his handy .38 Smith and Wesson and yelled profanities at the passenger. He never left the house without his S&W pistol.)

My family was nervous about Daddy being attacked when he was driving his cab. My father did not put much stock in banks and, therefore, kept most of his money in his shirt pocket. We were concerned that he would be robbed. Both shirt pockets were usually filled to the brim with money, notes, and pens. He was a little on the eccentric side about things like that.

Daddy loved to tell tall tales, and each time a story was told it was embellished a little more. He also had a tremendous imagination and loved to describe events from when he was a boy living in poverty. I cannot begin to count the number of times that I heard him tell of drinking water out of a mule track when he was young.

My wife describes Daddy by calling him quite a "character." I must agree that he truly was.

Dad with one of his taxis

The Wildcat Roller Coaster at Joyland Park

Joyland Park

nyone remember Joyland Park in Lexington? I can fondly remember when I was old enough to move from the "kiddy-land" rides at the popular park to the adult attractions, such as the Wildcat roller coaster. It was a thrill to share the day there with a special friend and enjoy the rides. Somehow being there could make you feel like you were older and more independent than you really were.

Joyland Park was in operation in Lexington from 1926 until it closed in 1964. It was located on Paris Pike. My first visit to the park occurred when my Uncle Charles took me with his family when I was around seven years old.

My Aunt Ruth prepared a picnic lunch, but I was so excited that I hardly had any appetite. The sound of the Merry-Go-Round organ playing the "oom-pa-pa" tune and the smell of the various food vendors made it impossible to concentrate on Aunt Ruth's picnic goodies.

Uncle Charles and Aunt Ruth sat in one of the Merry-Go-Round bench seats behind their daughter, Janis, and me as we rode the painted ponies. Janis and I both were so disappointed when the ride stopped and we had to get off in order for someone else to get on our horses.

While I was a student at Mt. Vernon High School, it was customary for the freshman class to go to Joyland Park during the second semester, just before school closed for the summer. I vividly remember boarding the bus with my classmates to make the trip up US 25 (no interstate road in those days) to spend the day enjoying the rides, eating all the fair-like treats, and just being together having fun.

All the way along the route to Lexington, we sang continuously, "99 Bottles of Beer on the Wall" – much to the dismay of the poor bus driver and our accompanying chaperones. One of the ladies said, "Don't you all know any other songs?"

Weeks before the trip, the guys would choose a special girl who would agree to ride the amusement park rides as his date. I recall being in a group with Carla, Sandy, Gary, Marion, and Charlotte, as we stood in line for the Tilt-A-Whirl. It was one of the most popular rides – along with the Octopus, Bump-um cars, the Merry-Go-Round, and, of course, The Wildcat.

The guys in my class were thrilled to get into one of the Bumper cars with that special girl and ride for what seemed like hours, slamming into a car with another guy and his "date." I suppose we were pretending that the cars were actually "hot-rods" and that we were old enough to drive.

The old wooden roller-coaster, called The Wildcat, was one of the hallmarks of Joyland. You could hear the beams creak and sway as the ride slowly climbed up the track and then dived to the ground on the other side. The girls squealed with both delight and fear as the car rocked back and forth each time we started over the next hump.

By the end of the day, we were tired and could barely get back on the bus waiting to take us home. Instead of singing and yelling, most of us slept all the way back to Mt. Vernon. The day was one of great adventure, fun, and bonding with our classmates.

When I graduated from high school and moved to Lexington to attend UK, lots of weekends were spent at Joyland. They had a great swimming pool and also had dancing on weekends. In those days, big name rock-and-roll bands would perform for large crowds on Saturday nights. It was a cool place to take a date and dance the night away.

When Joyland Park closed in 1964 it was disquieting to lots of teens as well as many of their parents. The bygone amusement park had been enjoyed by visitors from all over Kentucky and from adjoining states. Its memory lives on in the minds of countless former park attendees – including mine.

The Joyland Club at Joyland Park

Lightning Strikes Again!

When I was very young and living with my mother and grandparents on our hilltop farm in Rockcastle County, I was taught to be terribly afraid of storms. Both my mother and grandmother were terrified of lightning. Once a storm appeared on the horizon, we were shuffled to the living room to sit on the couch or to the cellar to wait for it to pass. To a young impressionable boy, it taught alarm, dread, and fear.

Our farm had lots of very old trees (oak and poplar), and many of these were located in our yard. It was common to see lightning hit one of these tall, stately trees and explode it into pieces of charred mulch scattered all over the place. I suppose because we lived on the top of a hill and because the trees were so old, they were good targets for lightning. I have always heard that you should avoid tall trees in a storm. Believe me, you never had to remind me of that when I was little.

When lightning struck something close to our house, both of these "Nervous Nellies" that I lived with would scream and flinch as if they themselves had been hit. When the storm approached, all electrical appliances were turned off or even unplugged. That meant that we could not listen to the radio or (heaven forbid) the television. The antenna was even disconnected from the TV!

I will never forget one afternoon when lightning actually hit the fuse box in the kitchen, which was located on the wall behind the couch. Blue light raced through the house while pieces of the fuse box flew all over the kitchen. Well, that was the beginning of our trips to the cellar. From that point on, we moved quickly underground whenever a storm approached and stayed locked inside until no thunder could be heard.

That tiny room was filled with canned vegetables, sacks of potatoes, onions, and other items that my grandfather stored inside. It was damp and very dark. I hated sitting in there with a kerosene lantern as the only source of light or heat. It had the typical musty smell, and I remember crickets scampering all around while we waited for the storm to pass. When lightning hit close by, Mommie Katie would exclaim, "Lordy – Lordy!"

It was during that time that I started taking a flashlight with me every time we ventured into the cellar. Me, my transistor radio, and my trusty flashlight sitting with two hysterical women and my grandfather. It is not one of my favorite memories!

We had a neighbor who was in the Navy. One weekend when he was on furlough, he taught me how to determine how far away a storm was. He said, "Watch for the lightning and count how many seconds it takes before you hear the thunder. That is how many miles the storm is from you." From that point on, I was counting to see if the storm was coming toward us or moving away. I kept counting – and I still do!

As a teenager, I learned that being in an automobile was the safest place to be in an electrical storm. Fine, I thought, I will be sure to be in my car when the next storm approaches. That was all well and good until one night when I had a date for the drive-in theatre. As we were driving to the movie, a lightning bolt hit a tree directly in front of my car. The tree exploded right in front of our eyes! I thought to myself, "Am I doomed to be killed by lightning?" My date was so frightened that she wanted me to take her home. My only reaction was, "Lightning strikes again!"

A few years later, several of my college friends and I rented a houseboat on Lake Cumberland for the weekend. We loaded all of our supplies and gear onto that huge boat and headed for a secluded spot far away from civilization. After we tied the boat to some overhanging trees and unpacked our "stuff," I noticed a small dark cloud on the horizon. Paying no attention to the weather, my friends began to swim, fish, and eat. I kept watching that cloud. About 4 o'clock it started to thunder. By 5 o'clock it was raining, and lightning was all around us. We started up the small motor and headed back to the dock -- which we did not make before a full-blown storm was upon us. Lightning was striking in every direction and the wind began to blow like mad. I felt as though I was on the Titanic! Much to my relief, we finally reached the dock and arrived safely on land. It stormed all weekend, and the most we did was sit on the boat and play cards at the dock. "Lightning strikes again!"

When my wife and I married, I was alarmed to learn that she loved watching lightning and would stand in an open door to witness it playing in the distance. She has had a hard time convincing me that the fireworks associated with storms are actually very beautiful and fun to watch. (I still insist that the doors and windows are closed when an electrical storm is in the vicinity of our home.) Fortunately, our home on Furnace Mountain provides a large picture window to view lightning shows from quite a distance. I am grateful for the influence my wife has played on my opinion of electrical storms. However, my first inclination is still to respond to storms the way my two shelties (Jesse and Cody) do – take cover!

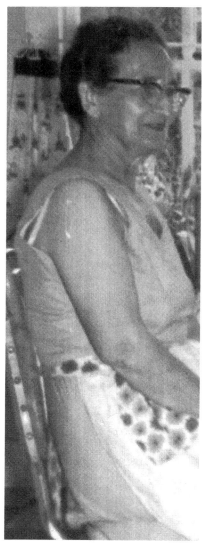

Mommie Katie in her apron

Mommie Katie's Apron

A few weeks ago, I noticed that my wife was ironing – a chore that she almost never performs. (She promised to love, honor, and cherish – but not to iron.) As a matter of fact, we could almost get along without an iron; we don't even own an ironing board. Therefore, my curiosity got the best of me, and I just had to find out what prompted the ever-so-rare ironing she was doing. Upon looking closer, I saw that she was pressing several of her mother's vintage aprons.

You may not know it, but aprons are "in" again, and particularly so if they are old ones from the good ole days. Upon my mother-in-law's death, several old aprons were found. A couple of them – one belonging to my wife's mother and the other to her grandmother – were kept as keepsakes.

But most of the other ones were somewhat delicate and ornate. When I asked why she was washing and ironing the protective garments, she explained that she was giving them to our friend Mimi. It is a perfect fit. Half the time Mimi looks like she stepped right out of the sixties anyway, and she is also a young mother who sees the practical use of an apron when cooking and serving.

At about the same time that I found my wife ironing, one of my high school friends (Mattie Burton Petrey) sent me an e-mail about how the apron was used in the 1950s. I took this as I sign that I should write about my grandmother's daily use of these fine pieces of apparel.

Mommie Katie donned her apron as soon as she got dressed in the morning. The principal use was, of course, to protect her dresses while she prepared the family meals. But that was hardly the only use for these garments. I am sure that I will not be able to explain thoroughly the many ways that she put them to use; however, I will try to demonstrate their valuable nature.

The first thing that comes to mind is how Mommie Katie used her apron as a potholder to lift hot items from the wood-burning kitchen stove. She daily prepared a large pot of very strong coffee, which was aged on the stove throughout the morning and early afternoon. Each time she finished her cup of brew, the apron was used to lift the pot from the stove to pour another cup. It was also used to remove extremely hot, iron baking pans from the oven, especially her famous cornbread muffin pans.

Aprons were used outdoors as well as in the kitchen. I have watched Mommie in the early morning as she gathered eggs from the hen house, placing them in her apron to bring in and cook for breakfast. Or she might fill it with kindling when she started to build a fire before cooking. Sometimes she filled her apron with strings or hulls when she broke fresh half-runner green beans.

From the garden, her apron was filled with all sorts of vegetables, such as tomatoes, radishes, cucumbers, or even corn. After she hulled the corn or peeled the other vegetables, the apron was used to carry the waste products to the edge of the garden for disposal.

In the fall, that same apron was used to bring in apples, peaches, and pears for canning or preparing those wonderful cobblers. It was also used for transporting her beautiful flowers into the house in order for her to put them into vases to decorate our home.

That big old apron was used on many occasions to wipe away the tears of a growing boy and to clean surplus grime from our faces. Once I remember her using it to clean a bicycle scrape from my knee. She was even known to clean our ears with the hem!

When my mother or Pop announced that company was pulling into the driveway, Mommie Katie used that big old apron to make a few swipes in the living room to wipe away the dust that had accumulated on her furniture. She could dust a whole room in a matter of seconds when company was walking up the lawn.

I also remember her wiping away the perspiration from her brow with her apron when she was working in her flower garden. Everyone in the neighborhood agreed that her flowers were the finest in the area, and she worked hard to keep them free from weeds and insects.

Mommie Katie's apron was a large part of who she was, and she used it for a wide variety of daily chores. Except for Sunday morning and Wednesday night when she attended church, it hung from her waist ready for an assortment of uses.

Most ladies of those days found aprons to be invaluable aids for cleaning, carrying, and wiping. As a matter of fact, when I picture Mommie in my mind's eye, it is always with an apron on. It was a major part of who she was.

No wonder I found my wife ironing aprons – it was a labor of love.

Old-fashioned apron

Pop

Pop's Push Mower

I had a chat recently with Kevin, a young man who takes care of my lawn and yard work. Kevin does a great job, but he has lots of riding equipment that probably cost him a king's ransom. A turn in the conversation reminded me of my grandfather and his push reel mower. He taught me to use it when I was only about nine years old.

Pop and Mommie Katie had a large yard to mow that was nearly an acre. Pop's only means of maintaining a well-kept yard was the reel mower and a small hand scythe. He did not yet trust me with the scythe, so I was trained to push the mower. The chore literally took the entire day to complete.

The day began with Mommie Katie serving us a good ole country breakfast, which by very definition includes home-made biscuits and gravy. Afterwards, Pop would proceed to remind me how long the unpleasant task was going to take and then simply said, "Come on, David Joe. Let's get to mowing."

While I struggled to push the cylinder mower to cut the grass, Pop used the scythe to trim the edges around the yard as well as around all of Mommie Katie's flowers. Occasionally, he came over and suggested that I let him "spell me." (If you are unfamiliar with the language, it is an old-fashioned term meaning to take someone's place in his stead. In other words, he was relieving me of the task for a spell.)

It was then that I would get a tall glass of iced tea prepared by Mommie Katie for her working men. I can tell you that no iced tea could ever taste as good as hers did – most especially when taking a break from mowing. Sitting under a shade tree drinking that refreshing concoction, I watched Pop push the manual mower and wipe away the perspiration flowing from his brow.

As soon as I was finished with my glass of tea, I again took the mower from Pop to continue until it was time to take another break. We took turns pushing the manual mower until the yard met his expectations.

Pop took great pride in the completed project. At the end of the day, he often asked me to join him under his favorite tree. He paid me 50 cents per hour for my labor. In those days, that was a very valuable job for a young boy to have.

My older brother, Al, has a story that he tells on himself which involves Pop's hand scythe. Evidently, Mommie Katie was chasing Al for something he had done when she noticed the scythe laying in the yard. As she ran by it, she scooped it up and continued after him. Al looked back with horror when he discovered that she was coming after him with the blade in her hand. He cried out, "Mommie, you will kill me with that thing!" Mommie got so tickled that the chase could not continue because she was laughing so hard.

When I was about 12, Pop decided to replace the push mower. He purchased a brand new Briggs and Stratton gasoline-powered machine. I thought that was the greatest invention ever made! We continued to share the mowing chore, but the time it took was actually cut in half. Pop and I could manicure the entire yard in just a few hours.

Each week before we began, Pop would turn the new mower on its side. He used his large file to make certain that the blades were sharp enough to cut the yard to his specifications. He made me hold the machine until the blades were ready for the mowing.

Again, it was my job to cut the grass while he completed the trimming. Oh, how much easier it was to finish my assigned task! You might say that I fell in love with that gas-powered mower.

There was another custom that usually followed the completion of yard mowing. After the job was completed and we had taken our baths, Pop loved to drive down to Cummins Grocery to get a cold watermelon for us to eat in the backyard.

When choosing just the right one, he got out his pocket knife to "plug" the melon to see whether it was ripe. (Can you imagine doing that today at a grocery store?) When he finally selected one to his satisfaction, we placed it in his car and drove home.

Once we arrived, we enjoyed the sweet treat while sitting in lawn chairs in the shady backyard. I can see Pop now sitting slumped over a large slice of cold melon, spitting the seeds into the yard.

As I have observed before, life in those days was much less complicated. Harder, maybe, but there is something to be said for the plain life. There was a particular satisfaction in its down-to-earth work and the simple pleasures that accompanied it.

An old-fashioned purse like Mommie Katie's

Mommie Katie's Pocketbook

My grandmother always referred to her purse as her "pocketbook," and she used that term often. All of her life she was a stay-at-home housewife who maintained her home exquisitely. Her home was her castle, and she alone was completely in charge. One large chest of drawers in the guest bedroom was filled with her "unmentionables," and in the very back of that same drawer, she kept her big old pocketbook well hidden. No one else ever opened that drawer, and none of us was actually sure of what she kept hidden there.

Mommie Katie was always coming up with new ideas to position her furniture, even that special chest of drawers. Sometimes after the rest of the family was fast asleep, she would get out of bed and re-arrange the furniture in one room or another. You never knew where things were to be found when you got out of bed for breakfast. It was her beloved domicile, and she wanted it to be just as she desired. About the only items that were secure were the living room couch and the easy chairs, because they always were pointed toward the television. It had to be located close to the antenna, which was positioned on the roof of the house.

As the breadwinner of the family, my grandfather customarily gave Mommie Katie cash each time he received a check from Aubry Feed Mills or Louisville Grocery, where he worked for over forty years. Of course, none of us ever knew how much he gave her each month – nor did we even consider asking about it. We just knew that each time he handed her money, she quietly walked to the guest bedroom and pulled out that old pocketbook.

Mommie Katie used her "stash" for her own purposes; there was never a discussion about it. After many years of observation, the rest of the family knew that she used most of that money for gifts, charity, and her weekly tithe to the First Baptist Church of Mt. Vernon.

It was long-established that the pastor of our church would come home with the family after Sunday services; it was relatively rare for this not to occur. Of course, he also made home visits regularly. And every time he was ready to leave, Mommie Katie would exclaim, "Don't leave yet!" She then made her way to that chest of drawers, and as she shook his hand goodbye, she discreetly handed him some cash. She never made a spectacle out of it; she simply wadded up a handful of cash and placed it into his hand. Even Pop knew not ask how much money she gave to the pastor on his visits to our home.

When I became a teenager, Mommie Katie consistently kept herself aware of my needs at that most important stage of life. When she noticed that I was getting ready for a date, she would ask, "David Joe, do you need some money for your date?" Of course, my answer was usually the same – that I could sure use it. She would then proceed to retrieve her pocketbook and out came a "secret amount" of cash.

She always gave me the same orders: "Here, put this in your pocket and don't tell anyone!" When she handed me bills, they were always wadded up; so I would quickly pocket it and give her a big hug. As soon as the exchange was complete, she always said, "Now you be careful." The whole deal was kept our secret because that is the way Mommie Katie wanted it. Only after I had gotten into my car did I check to see just how much she had given me. Usually it amounted to fifteen or twenty dollars – no small sum in those days!

You don't hear the term "pocketbook" much anymore – and if you do, it will absolutely be some elderly woman to utter it. Therefore, whenever I hear that word or even see it written, Mommie Katie immediately pops into my mind. I don't think she ever allowed anyone to leave her home hungry or needing a small amount of cash. I believe that she was the most generous person I ever met.

When I was preparing to leave Mt. Vernon to attend college at the University of Kentucky, Mommie Katie took me for a walk into the woods behind her house. I could not help but notice that she brought along her big old pocketbook on our walk, so I was pretty sure of what she had in mind. When we had ventured far enough to be out of sight of anyone, she reached into that big old purse and handed me a small roll of cash. She instructed me, "Put some of this away for emergencies and use the rest when you need a good meal." We hugged there in those woods, and a tear rolled down my cheek because I knew she was making a sacrifice because she loved me so much. Even when she was older, she would tell my mother, "Ruby, get me my pocketbook. David Joe needs some cash."

Every time I came home from UK, Mommie Katie made sure that we took a walk in the yard before I returned to Lexington. She never failed to send me back to school without some cash in my jeans pocket. She always asked, "Is there anything special that you need this time?" I would let her know if there was something unusual going on at UK.

It seems strange to me now that the use of the word "pocketbook" can bring back such fond recollections of my wonderful grandmother. She was one of the most dedicated Christian women that I have ever known. She made a tremendous difference in my life, and for that I will always be thankful. Her Christian influence followed me all the rest of my life. And I could never forget the times she "bailed" me out of financial problems as a young man. Even after she has been gone all these many years, I still miss her presence in my life – and I don't mean just her pocketbook.

Mommie Katie and Pop

Small Town Southern Man

*A*nyone who has followed my column understands just how much my grandfather meant to me. Another recent music purchase (I just can't help myself) again reminded me of him and his influence on my life.

A few days ago, I bought Alan Jackson's most recent CD entitled *Good Times*. Apparently, the most popular song on it is Small Town Southern Man, because it is getting a lot of play time on local country radio stations. The song describes Pop in vast detail. The first time I carefully listened to my new CD, tears filled my eyes as the memory of Pop came flooding back.

> *Born the middle son of a farmer*
> *And a small town Southern man,*
> *Like his daddy's daddy before him*
> *Brought up workin' on the land.*
> *Fell in love with a small town woman*
> *And they married up and settled down;*
> *Natural way of life if you're lucky*
> *For a small town Southern man.*

Pop was definitely a small town southern man. He and his family before him spent all their lives working small farms producing vegetables and meat for their families. Pop originally lived in the small community called Hopewell in Rockcastle County. When he took me to see the specific site where he had lived, we had to traverse a small creek in order to get to his old home place.

Callous hands told the story
For this small town Southern man
He gave it all to keep it all together
And keep his family on his land.
Like his daddy, years wore out his body
Made it hard just to walk and stand;
You can break the back
But you can't break the spirit
Of a small town Southern man

Even during the Great Depression, Pop worked hard and maintained his small farm in Rockcastle County. I never witnessed anyone who worked as hard or knew as much about farm life as Pop. I cannot remember him taking a day off from his chores. There was something that had to be done every day.

Pop eventually developed a hernia from the lifting and digging on the farm. It was never discussed as to whether he should slow down or have surgery for his problem. His answer was to purchase a truss and keep on working. Arthritis also became a significant physical problem for him, but he refused to take medications for the pain.

And he bowed his head to Jesus
And he stood for Uncle Sam
And he only loved one woman
He was always proud of what he had.
He said his greatest contribution
Is the ones you leave behind
Raised on the ways and gentle kindness
Of a small town Southern man

Pop was a Christian man who served in the Mt. Vernon Baptist Church. He was the church treasurer and was adamant that every penny was accounted for in this position. He was also a man of honor when it came to his country. His political affiliation was Republican, and he never budged from his dedication. He considered it an honor to vote in every election.

When he met Mommie Katie, who was definitely a small town woman, he fell in love with her and they were married until he died. It was nothing but natural for him to live with his first love for over 50 years.

Pop could be gruff, but inside was a very gentle and loving person. He instilled in his family this gentle nature.

> *Finally death came callin'*
> *For this small town Southern man.*
> *He said, "It's alright 'cause I see angels*
> *And they got me by the hand.*
> *Don't you cry, and don't you worry,*
> *I'm blessed, and I know I am,*
> *'Cause God has a place in Heaven*
> *For a small town Southern man."*

Pop influenced my life in ways that I still find remarkable. Integrity, truthfulness, and a love of God were considered the basic ways of life to Pop. Throughout my adult life, I have found that my values reflect his directions. As I have said before, Pop provided me with skills, principles, and values which have served me well and remain part of my life's philosophy. I loved him unconditionally. And I know that he is waiting for his family on the other side.

Commercial Chicken House

The Chicken House

When people learn how many different kinds of jobs I have worked over the years, the term "jack of all trades" usually surfaces. It is true that I have been blessed all of my life with a variety of jobs that I have loved. And I am thankful that I have always had the physical and mental ability to work. My parents and grandparents taught me to work hard and be self sufficient. I started as a young boy with chores like mowing the lawn, for which my grandfather would pay me 50 cents an hour. It was good training. I wanted the grass to grow faster so I could earn more spending money.

But there was one chore that I will admit I could never love. I was reminded of the experience while watching television when a commercial came on showing the inside of a chicken house. Immediately, my thoughts returned to my high school days when I worked for my father tending his chickens. Now let me tell you, I may have enjoyed nearly every job I ever had, but I detested working in that chicken house.

Dad had 13,000 chickens housed in three different buildings. A meat packing plant would deliver the baby chicks, and we fed them for nine weeks. It was my duty each morning to feed those nasty animals. Chickens are very dusty because of their feathers and the sawdust they walk on, not to mention that they fill the floor with their droppings. Each day I would carry bags of feed throughout these houses and dump it into feeders hanging from the roof. Back and forth I would go until all 13,000 were fed.

When finished, I was a sight to behold – covered from top to toe with feathers, dust, and worst of all, chicken manure. I couldn't wait to get home and soak in the shower before heading out to school. Because my mother felt sorry for me, she would have a feast on the table when I got out of the shower.

After about nine weeks, my father would tell me to hire about a dozen high school boys and meet him at the chicken houses at dark. This meant that it was time to ship the chickens to the meat-packing plant.

We were instructed to put nine chickens in each coop and then load them on the truck. After giving us our orders, Dad would turn off all the lights. You see, the birds had never seen darkness because we wanted them to eat 24 hours a day. As soon as the lights went out, the chickens would flop down on the floor as if they had died. It was very bizarre. We would walk through the houses picking up three chickens in each hand and take them to the coops. (Even as I write, that horrible smell comes back to me too clearly.)

After filling a coop, it was hauled over to the tractor trailer and hoisted up to the driver. He had weighed the truck before we filled it with chickens, and he would weigh it again when it was full. At that time, my father was paid five cents per pound for the chickens. My nine weeks of feeding and helping to load the truck would finally pay off.

I was so glad to see them drive off. I wanted to follow the truck just to make sure that he didn't bring them back! Dad always took a couple of weeks to clean the houses before more chickens were delivered, so I could sleep in for a few days. That is, until the next load of chickens arrived…

Man that had to be the worst job I ever had. I suppose if that is true, then I have been a very lucky guy. Nevertheless, that's one job I wouldn't wish onto my worst enemy.

A Warm Morning stove similar to the one my family had.

The Warm Morning Stove

While sitting in front of the fireplace in my den reading the Sunday *Lexington Herald-Leader*, I started to watch the flicker of the fire. It reminded me of my childhood days when we had a large, Warm Morning stove in the den of my grandfather's house. That stove had a small window in the front panel which allowed you to see the flames that were dancing inside.

Pop was the lone keeper of the fire. He had perfected the art of fire building and making it last for hours on end. No one else was permitted to add coal or even to use the poker in order to stir up the coals. Pop took this job seriously and tended to it with masterful attention.

Before retiring for the evening, Pop would adjust the damper on the stove pipe, set the draft on the bottom door, and place just the right amount of coal inside for the fire to last all night long. The next morning all he had to do was make a few adjustments and that Warm Morning stove would make the house feel "toasty" warm. He was proud of his fire-making skills.

We had another small, coal-burning stove in the kitchen. It was used to heat that part of the house and to heat the water for the water heater. Mommie Katie only allowed coal to be placed in two coal buckets which were hidden from view behind the stove in the kitchen. She was very emphatic about where coal could be stored inside the house.

On cold winter nights, Pop made a roaring fire in the stove in the den, pulled his cherry rocker up to the front of the stove, and rocked as he listened to his big, floor-model, wooden radio. It wasn't long until we could hear him snoring away in his contented state. He was at home, warm, and satisfied.

These two stoves were centrally located so that most of the rooms received the effect of their warmth. My bedroom, however, was positioned at the far corner of the house and did not get warm air from either of these sources of heat. I can remember a couple of times when I awoke to find a small skim of ice on the top of a glass of water at my bedside. Let me tell you, it is a rude awakening when it is that cold in your room. It was doubly difficult to get out of bed before the fires had warmed the house. In winter, I usually slept in athletic socks and PJ bottoms. I kept a sweatshirt hanging on the head post of my bed to put on before crawling out.

On nights that held the potential for extreme drops in temperature, my mother would place a couple of bricks on the top of the Warm Morning stove to warm them. She then wrapped them in a towel and positioned them under the covers at the foot of my bed. Placing my feet against warm towels was very comforting when it was particularly cold in my room. I would lie there listening to my transistor radio until I fell asleep under the stack of quilts that Bee had made. Sometimes the stack would be so heavy that it was nearly impossible to even turn over, but it kept me warm.

By the age of ten or eleven, I was assigned the task of filling the coal buckets before it got dark. The coal pile was located on the back corner of the yard next to the chicken house. Pop kept an old, rusty, chipped hatchet near the coal pile to break up the larger pieces into smaller blocks that would fit into the buckets. If we were expecting snow or very cold weather, Pop would instruct me to gather an extra bucket or two and set them next to the kitchen door.

Even though it is much easier today to deal with winter temperatures, I still miss the warmth, smell, and sounds of that great Warm Morning stove crackling in the den of our small farmhouse.

After visiting these wonderful memories of my childhood, I picked up my paper, returning to the news of the modern world as I sipped my coffee. In a few minutes, my wife would call me to come get some of her awesome scrambled eggs – for which she is very thankful that she does not have to prepare on a coal-burning stove.

Me with my brother, Al

Growing
Pains

Gene Autry

My Heroes Have Always Been Cowboys

My heroes have always been cowboys.
And they still are, it seems.
Willie Nelson

When I was a small boy, my world often revolved around pretending to be a cowboy with two six-shooters in leather holsters strapped on my side. I perched on the end of the couch, watching my heroes capture the bad guys on television. From that spot I could ride with my favorite "cow punchers" in their conquest of evil in the old west. I assisted Gene Autry, Hopalong Cassidy, Johnny MacBrown, and Lash LaRue in a variety of western adventures. I occasionally was shot out of the saddle and fell to the floor in my living room. Being a living room cowboy was dangerous business!

It was easy to determine who the bad guys were on television because of their black hats. Good cowpokes dressed in white hats and always won over evil. They could kill 40-50 bandits or Indians without even re-loading their six shooters. By watching these adventures on TV, we learned to be courteous and how to fight for what was right.

Most of the heroes were loners, with relationships only with their horses – or possibly a side-kick (such as Walter Brennan, Fuzzy St. John, or Gabby Hayes). They slept on the ground with a trusty horse watching over them. A good fire and a pot of coffee were all they required to feel comfortable while on the job in the Wild West. One of my favorites was a character named Lash LaRue. His special talent was the use of a bullwhip in his pursuit of outlaws. I talked my grandfather into letting me get a whip of my own. I practiced the art of "lashing" a pistol out of the hand of bad guys. I wasn't too bad! Lash was also different in how he dressed. He opted for the black outfit to go along with his black horse, aptly named Black Diamond. He played alongside a very funny side-kick named Fuzzy Q. Jones.

All of the young cowboys in my neighborhood rode the range on their "tobacco stick" horses. Because of my fondness for Lash, I painted mine black like Black Diamond and tied a white scarf around his neck to resemble the white mane. We were quite a sight! Several of the boys in my neck of the woods gathered on Saturday to ride our "horses" into the woods in search of outlaws. We often used up several boxes of caps in our six-shooters as we tamed the frontier.

A neighbor gentleman who used Bull Durham smoking tobacco would save the small white pouches so that we could fill them with sand and pretend that we were transporting gold through the woods. Once we found a small wooden box, filled it with the bags of "gold," and buried it in the woods. To my knowledge, it was never retrieved. (Can you imagine the look on the face of a treasure hunter who eventually finds the "gold"?)

Pop also loved western movies. Almost every weekend, he took me to the Saturday matinee at the Vernon Theatre. Those were the days when the wheels of the wagons spun backward in the old black and white cowboy thrillers.

We usually sat through a Western double-feature. Pop loved the singing cowboys, such as Roy Rogers and Gene Autry, and knew most of the lyrics to the "fireside" songs. One of the reasons that he may have loved Westerns so much was because the good guys always saved the cattle ranch and won the favor of the girl.

Even today I still love a good western movie or TV show. My wife and I especially liked the series "Lonesome Dove." The main character was played by our favorite, Robert Duvall. He has the ability to make you feel that you are really part of the story. I always watch any western in which he plays a part.

I suspect that I will always be a fan of good western movies.

It reminds me of the hit song of The Statler Brothers in which they expressed how they felt about old western movies, "What Ever Happened to Randolph Scott?"

> *What ever happened to Randolph Scott,*
> *   riding the trail alone?*
> *Whatever happened to Gene and Tex and Roy and Rex,*
> *   the Durango Kid?*
> *What ever happened to Johnny Mac Brown?*
> *   ...Whatever happened to Lash LaRue?*
> *I'd love to see them again*
> *Whatever happened to all of these*
> *Has happened to the best of me.*

Hopalong Cassidy

Being a Child in the 50s

*I*n 1954, I was only ten years old, and this old world was a very different place. It is hard to believe that so many years have passed. We survived without many of the items that are now considered to be either essential or required by law. I recently tried to imagine what a shock it would be to go back to that time. Travel with me…as we consider how our lives have changed and how simple it was in the 50s.

My first bicycle: It was a 24-inch, orange bike with no fenders. Nothing fancy about it. We had never heard of wearing a helmet, and we could ride with a friend sitting on the crossbar. Its paint was probably lead-based. Of course, we wedged a baseball card in the spokes so that the bike was transformed into a "motorcycle." We went everywhere on our bikes. We rode all day long and never considered being tired – or staying inside to play. The world was our playground. It would have been considered punishment if we had to stay cooped up inside the house.

When we got thirsty, we simply turned on the garden hose and got our fill. Our water came from a well in the yard. It contained no fluoride and was not treated in any way. Paying for water in plastic bottles would never have occurred to us. The water from our well was free. If we were fortunate enough to have a soft drink, we shared it with two or three friends…without considering diseases that we might pass from one to another.

If we went for a ride in the family car, there were no seat belts or air bags. We physically "rolled down" the windows, and our arms waved in the breeze rushing past. Occasionally, a hand would be smacked by a passing bug. In my hometown, the entire family drove to town on Saturday night and parked the car on the street. We watched people. We watched to see who drove by our car. Just before going home, my grandfather bought all of us an ice cream cone – to cool us off before going to bed.

Children from the neighborhood gathered in our yard to play in the evening. We knew each other by name, and so did our parents. We played hide and seek, kick the can, and marbles. We climbed trees. Every boy had a BB gun and knew how to use it safely. Sometimes the girls brought their dolls and played in a group, while the boys went on adventures with their air rifles. The weapon used most often between the children was a trusty water balloon.

No one was ever seriously injured. And no one ever got sued. Parents in the neighborhood could and would discipline the kids who were playing in their yards. That was essential – an unspoken rule that both adults and children understood.

None of us had television sets, much less video games. Nor had we ever heard of FM radio. Phones were mounted on the wall, and nearly the entire community was on "party" lines. At our house, we only answered the phone when it rang three short rings. If it was any other sort of ring, it was for someone else.

We had never heard of tape decks, and computers were room-sized machines for large businesses or colleges. Hardware was nuts and bolts, saws, hammers, and axes. No one had ever heard of "software."

None of our homes contained air conditioners, dishwashers, or electric blankets. At night, we slept with only the screen doors closed to keep animals out and let the night air in. We never locked our doors. We slept with no fear of intruders coming into our homes. Cigarette smoking was the thing to do, and almost every adult smoked. Penicillin had not even been developed. The polio vaccine was just being introduced into our school systems. A nurse came to school to give injections to every child. Contact lenses had not been invented.

We ate bread with real butter. Food was flavored with bacon drippings (lard), and meat was present on the table for every meal. We licked the bowl when our mothers made cakes containing real eggs. Who ever thought of getting salmonella poisoning? Because we played outdoors in our yards, fields, and forests all day long, very few children were overweight. We simply ran off the excess calories.

It is refreshing to remember the simplicity of that era. What I would give to sit for a few hours on our old front porch in the swing with my grandparents! Or to walk with Pop through our garden, watching him pull turnips from the patch and pealing them with his pocket knife. I can see him holding a slice for me to sample. I long to stroll with Mommie Katie through the apple orchard or through her flower garden. What a thrill it was to watch my mother make sauerkraut in our back yard as she chopped fresh cabbage from our garden.

OK...OK...I know that modern conveniences are wonderful, and we probably would not want to return to the 50s. No one today would want to live without his air conditioning, million-channel TV, or his power tools. We wouldn't be comfortable in a world without access to daily showers and the modern plumbing that accommodates all of those work-saving appliances.

Nevertheless, the 50s had much to offer. The era provided many of us with a touchstone to the identity of family, of community, and of self – secured upon values of trust and responsibility. I failed to realize how fortunate I was to be growing up at such a time. It all played out in a way that resulted in us living in a kind of affluence that we didn't know we had.

Boyhood Slingshot

When I was a young boy, my grandfather chose, as a form of entertainment, to teach me how to construct a slingshot. One of my friends had one, and I asked Pop to show me how to make a similar weapon to hunt small game and to target practice. Of course, he readily agreed and off to the woods we went to find just the right forked willow stick.

Pop found a willow shrub with a Y shaped limb, and he carefully removed the branch, leaving the plant to grow other limbs for future use. At once he sat down on a tree stump and made himself comfortable. He then began to whittle the willow limb to form the right size for a slingshot.

I was amazed to see the tool take shape as he worked. When he was finished, we took the branch back to Pop's tool shed and looked for an old inner tube to make the elastic portion of my new toy. With an old pair of scissors, he cut two pieces of rubber exactly the same size for the stretchy portion of the slingshot. He then proceeded to tie it in place with some string he had in his toolbox. Next, he cut a piece of leather from an old shoe tongue to serve as the projectile holder of the weapon.

I was so excited to watch the slingshot come together in Pop's hands. To me, he was a genius concerning such things. He could make a great number of useful items using only his knowledge and his tools.

After completing my slingshot, Pop was careful to explain to me that this was a dangerous weapon that could kill small game or put someone's eye out if it was not used correctly. He emphatically announced his rules about my new slingshot. I can remember him saying, "David Joe, you must never point this toward anyone or any animal that you do not intend to hurt or kill!" His instructions made an impact on me, and I never did point it toward anyone.

For the next few weeks I became a "big game hunter" and stalked trees, Coke cans, and some birds with my trusty weapon. Pop had told me that I could shoot at any Blue Jays, crows, or grackles when I located them. He explained that these birds destroyed the eggs of songbirds, and they could be eliminated when possible. I was excited to learn I could actually hunt some animals with my trusty weapon.

I actually went on game hunts in the Big Fill Cave area near our farm and was successful on a few occasions. One Saturday afternoon, Kenneth Hansel and I were hunting near the cave mouth and saw a large Jay harassing a bluebird nest. I was able to hit the Jay and chase it away. Pop said, "It will probably not come back now that you actually hit it."

My slingshot was actually too big to hide in my pocket so I got the bright idea to make another model that was much smaller and would fit in my back pocket. I wanted to have a concealed weapon any time it was needed. So I gathered some tools and possible items to use for the new slingshot and hid in my bedroom. For the handle I decided to use a heavy-duty wire coat hanger. I carefully used pliers to shape the handle to look like the willow handle that Pop had made out of wood. After cutting the wire and shaping the handle, it would fit in the palm of my hand.

My next move was to cut large rubber bands for the stretch portion of my miniature slingshot. I measured each band and tied them to the coat hanger. I also cut a small square piece of suede leather for the projectile holder. It, too, was tied to the rubber bands. I had decided to use BB's for my ammunition. Now I was ready to test my new toy.

I went out to Pop's backyard and set up a couple of Coke cans on fence posts and stepped back about 50 feet. To my surprise, the accuracy of my tiny slingshot was awesome. Out of the first ten BB's, I was able to hit the cans seven or eight times. I thought to myself, "This is great to be able to put this tiny slingshot in my back jeans pocket and have it ready when it is needed."

My father, Hobe, was operating the Mt. Vernon Hotel at the time, and he occasionally asked me to spend the weekend with him. That particular Friday night, Daddy allowed me to walk up and down Main Street with my friend Kenneth Hansel. We were casually looking into every window and watching the cool automobiles passing up and down the street. Just in front of the hotel, I saw a large blackbird sitting on an electrical line—and out came my trusty slingshot. I took careful aim and let go a BB toward the perching bird. The next thing I heard was a window breaking in an upper room of the hotel. I quickly tucked away my weapon and proceeded to casually walk on down the street.

That night when I went to my Dad's apartment in the hotel, he asked, "David Joe, did you see anyone with a BB gun when you were down on the street?" I replied that I had not. He said, "Someone shot out one of my windows a little while ago, and I did not see who it was." (I was telling mostly the truth because I did not see anyone with a BB gun. I never told him that I was responsible or showed him my miniature slingshot.)

Once again, I learned a valuable lesson. It was not very difficult to make trouble for yourself with a slingshot, so I had better heed the advice of Pop and try to be more responsible with my nifty toy weapon.

Let the Night Games Begin

When I was a youngster living with my grandparents, it was a custom to gather all the neighborhood children after dinner to play childhood games in our yard. Mommie Katie and Pop preferred an early dinner and that was alright with me – it gave me more time for games before bedtime.

In those days, we knew how to entertain ourselves. Our imaginations were limitless, but most of the games we played were common experiences to most anyone growing up during that era. For example, while it was light, we rode our bicycles and played marbles or Mumbly Peg (also called "Mumbledy" Peg by some).

Now, Mumbly Peg was a boy's game for sure. I never saw a girl play the game because it involved pocket knives. We usually picked out a nice shade tree in an area where the grass was cut close to the ground; there we formed a circle of boys sitting on the ground.

The object was to toss the knives in a variety of 24 ways to make the blade stick into the dirt. If you missed one of the tosses, then it was the next person's turn. After many tries, each of us would complete the tosses and the looser had to "chew the peg."

The winner prepared a wooden peg (made with a stick) about two inches long and pushed it into the ground. All players took turns "whacking" at the peg with the back side of the closed knife, until it was driven down to the surface of the ground. The loser had to lie on his belly and dig the peg out of the ground with his teeth. Usually the loser spent lots of time spitting out dirt until the peg was successfully removed. (Another reason why girls didn't play this game.)

After such a competition, we were ready for a snack. Sometimes we walked up the road to the gas station to buy a small Coke and a bag of peanuts. The peanuts were poured into the soft drink, yielding a most enjoyable concoction with a salty taste. Some of my friends purchased another combination that became a standard and which endures to this day: an RC Cola and a Moon Pie.

Occasionally, we stopped at a small orchard on our way back home and literally filled our pockets with juicy June apples for something to munch on later. As the song says, *"Oh, those were the days, my friends!"*

When darkness set in, it was time for a game of Kick the Can. This game is much like hide and seek, in which one player is "it" and the others run off to hide. The person who is "it" must find each of the hidden players and tag them. The tagged players then sit close to the tin can and wait for the others to be found. Any player who has not been caught can kick the can, setting all of the captured players free. If "it" catches all of the players, he or she wins. And the next go-'round continues.

On some evenings, we would take time from our games to catch June bugs. Boys would tie a string around their hind legs and watch them fly in dizzy circles above our heads. The girls usually caught fireflies (lightning bugs), which they secured in Mason jars to light up the yard. Anyway, all of us were chasing insects all over the place. (Why is it that kids like to do that? For some reason, it is always fun.) Pop used to encourage us. He'd say, "Let them catch all of the bugs they can."

About the time we had spun ourselves out, Mommie Katie would yell, "Come and get your Kool-Aid while it's cold!" Immediately, we stopped whatever we were doing and ran to satisfy our thirsts. She served those drinks in the brightly colored, aluminum, iced tea glasses that were so popular at that time.

Sometimes she also offered us home-made, chocolate chip cookies that she had prepared while the night games were being played. While we were enjoying our snacks, we sat on the edge of the high porch, listening to the adults tell stories. Then, all of a sudden, one of the children would yell, "It's time to play." And off we would go again!

There were also those evenings when we sat in a circle under a huge Mulberry tree in Pop's front yard to tell ghost stories. One of my friends, Kenneth Hansel, was especially good at this, and he usually managed to get us to the place where we were turning our heads to see if the "boogie man" was behind us.

That same big, old, Mulberry tree was a great tree for climbing. It had long, strong, spreading branches that we crawled upon. It was a great place to watch the other children as they played in our yard. I can't tell you how many hours I spent in that mature giant. Sometimes I climbed up in "my old friend" just to take note of the birds that shared my perch.

After our games had been in progress for quite some time, I dreaded to hear the call that would put it all to an end for the day. My mother or grandmother would yell, "David Joe, it is time to come in and get ready for bed!" I knew then that I must tell my friends that I had to go in and that they must go home, too.

Those night games from my childhood resulted in a child who was all sweaty and covered nearly head-to-toe with dirt. Before I knew it, I was in a warm, soapy bath, and then on to bed I went.

Those days in my yard are clear in my memory: the color of summer green everywhere, the smell of the grass, the touch of the earth, the girlish squeals, the refreshment of ice-cold Kool-Aid, and the company of friends and family while savoring those night games.

Blackberry Season

I have always loved blackberry cobbler. I remember picking blackberries when I was just a boy so the family could share the joy of cobbler dishes.

My mother and my grandmother always hired me and one of my friends (usually Kenneth Hansel) to pick blackberries for them. They made cobblers and also canned whole blackberries to use during the winter. We were probably only 10 years old at the time, but we considered this job to be highly important.

The ladies provided us with half-gallon (lard) buckets with a bale so we could get into the blackberry vines and gather the fruit. When the small containers were full, we poured them into larger buckets to transport back home for Bee and Mommie Katie to do their magic. Of course, we were warned to watch out for snakes and told to avoid "chiggers." Believe me; it was not necessary to caution me about snakes!

Kenneth and I kept an eye out for the blackberry vines all summer so we would know where to find the dark blue gems. My grandfather cultivated a few vines in fence rows on our small farm, so that is where we would start out on our adventure. Once those small vines were depleted, we moved on to other known sources in the neighborhood.

An additional source of the fruit was located on a neighbor's farm which was across the road from our house. It was there on the Vaughn property that most of the berries we picked were found. The property was across US 25 in front of our farm.

I also remember finding the berries on the gravel road leading to

Juanita Davis's house. It was a great spot because we could stand in the road and did not have to crawl into the vines to collect our bounty.

We dutifully carried bucket after bucket back to Bee and Mommie Katie, and they carefully washed and prepared the wonderful fruit. Kenneth always accused me of eating more than I placed in the buckets. When we came back home with the first load, Bee laughed and laughed at the berry juice that we had on our faces and our clothes.

We were paid handsomely for our efforts. I still remember that we received 50 cents each per gallon of berries. We could make several dollars in a single day of berry picking. In the 50s, that was a large sum of funds for a couple of little boys.

Mommie Katie always canned lots of quarts of blackberries so she would have an ample supply to make cobblers during the winter. She also canned both blackberry jam and jelly. Although it has been nearly 50 years since those wonderful days, I have never found any jam or jelly that could hold a candle to hers.

Her cobbler was known all over Mt. Vernon for its wonderful taste and texture. Even the pastor at the First Baptist Church was known to praise her dish from his pulpit. (She usually invited him to our house for Sunday dinner when she was having his favorite dessert.) She served her delicacy hot – straight from the oven – with vanilla ice cream piled on top. (My mouth is watering as I write this.)

My favorite time to savor her cobbler was as a midnight snack. I often would sneak into the kitchen in the middle of the night to fill a bowl to the brim. From there I headed to my room so that I could eat as I listened to my transistor radio. Yum, yum! God bless her, Mommie Katie always made enough for left-over treats.

The quart jars of berries were stored in the cellar along with her awesome jams and jellies. One wall was almost filled with the fruit. I don't know what I would give for just one more taste of that wonderful delight.

You know that banquet they speak about in heaven? I'm thinking that Mommie Katie's cobbler is bound to be a part of it.

Knuckle Down

Most of the boys I knew in elementary school played marbles on a daily basis. We could hardly wait until recess to rush out to the play-ground and "knuckle-down." Many of us carried our prize marbles in a cigar box which we kept in our possession at all times. We were always ready for a game! A boy in my neighborhood gauged his success as a shooter by the number of marbles in his collection. It was a real rush to win several marbles in a day's playing. After coming home in the evening you would count how many marbles you had gained that day.

The marbles were the brightly-colored cat-eyes, steelies (steel ball bearings), and the clay-colored taws. Usually, a taw was larger than a regular marble and was used as the "shooter." To begin a game, we drew a circle (about six feet in diameter) and placed five of our marbles in the center of the ring. Each player had to ante the same number of marbles before the game started. We stood on one side of the ring and "lagged" our shooters to the other side of the ring to see who would be the closest to the line. That person was first to "knuckle down" – which meant placing a shooter between your thumb and fore finger to begin playing.

We played "for keeps" – meaning that if you hit another's marble and knocked it out of the circle, then you put it in your box to keep. It was common to win 30-40 marbles in a single day. I remember having several hundred in my collection at one time.

I often wondered why girls did not participate in our games. I guess it was not "lady-like" to get on your knees and play in the dirt with a group of boys. It seemed that most of the girls were jumping rope or playing with their dolls instead. If they ever played a game while sitting on the ground, it was usually jacks.

My friend Kenneth Hansel was the best shot that I ever knew. He had a knack for shooting marbles that was unmatched in the neighborhood. When he "knuckled-down," many of the boys would pick up their marbles and wait for another player to come along. The risk of loss was just too great. Kenneth lived across the road from me, and we played together a lot. I learned many secrets from him about the art of marble shooting. For instance, you could wet the shooter before you squeezed it between your thumb and forefinger to make it shoot out quicker. This increased the velocity of the taw and gave it more force.

As we got older, our marble games became more sophisticated. We started playing "drop-box." This was a game where a hole was burned into the top of a cigar box (just slightly larger than a marble). Players held a marble at their waist to see if they could hit the hole. If successful, you had to give them five of your marbles. All missed marbles became the property of the cigar box owner. It was nothing to witness several boys standing around in a circle to watch a drop-box game. Some of our friends became experts at dropping.

When boys gathered at one of our houses, we compared the quantity of our marble collections and traded "taws" for regular marbles. A good taw could be traded for up to 10 or 12 regular marbles. Some of my friends were so proud of their "shooters" that they would carry them in their pockets to display to fellow marble players.

The following poem reminds me of my "marble-playing" days.

"The Winner"
By D. Lemie
Marbles are fun, to play in the sun.
Don't frown, draw a ring and knuckle down.
I won an "Immie," that's a gimmie.
Joe lost a "Lutz," now he feels like a clutz.
I won a "Steelie," from poor ole Willie,
He played for keeps, and now he weeps.

Then I won an "Aggie," that's not shabby.
I won a "Cloud," boy am I proud!
I got Sally's "Allies," Tommy's commies,
And all of Merle's "Swirls." Cause…
I'm a MIBSTER, a real cool HIPSTER!

The Transistor Radio

When I was about ten years of age, a revolution began in the world of electronics – the "transistor radio." This remarkable pocket-sized creation was the beginning of portable music. It was the perfect method for teenagers to listen to their newly forming music called rock and roll – no matter where they might be.

I will never forget seeing the first of these radios at a Western Auto Store on Main Street in Mt. Vernon, Kentucky. After hearing the amazing device, I was hooked. I made immediate plans to save my allowance and yard-mowing money in order to purchase my first of such electronic gadgets.

Two companies working together, Texas Instruments of Dallas, Texas, and Industrial Development Engineering Associates (I.D.E.A.) of Indianapolis, Indiana, were behind the unveiling of what they labeled the "Regency TR-1," the world's first commercially-produced transistor radio. Listeners were prone to hold the entire radio directly against the ear, in order to minimize the rather "tinny" sound of the small speakers. Most of the radios also came with an earphone jack and a single earphone that even then provided only mediocre-quality sound reproduction. (But we didn't care one bit about the quality of sound, I assure you.)

During the next few months, I stashed all of my funds in a small box located in my bedroom closet. Each week I counted my coins and bills trying to accumulate the ghastly price of $49.95 needed to purchase the Regency TR-1. It seemed like it took an eternity to save that much money, but finally I was able to gather my funds, walk into the Western Auto Store, and promptly tell the manager that I wanted to buy one of his special radios.

You have never seen anyone more proud of a purchase than I was at the time. I can remember the first night with it in my bedroom, holding the radio next to my ear as I turned the dial to locate the stations that I wanted to hear. It may seem silly now for such a small electronic device to be so exciting, but that is merely because we have all grown up in the age of quickly changing electronics. And it was this original one that really got the ball rolling for virtually everything else because of the very thing that made it so unique: the transistor.

With this new gadget, any individual could not only listen to the radio programming of his choice but could take it with him wherever he went. It allowed me to listen to my music far away from the adults in my family. I was in control of what I wanted to hear! I even took my new radio with me when I ventured into the woods near my home. The number of different stations that were available was limited only by the weather. If it was a crystal clear night, you could hear music from all over the country.

One night I heard Wolfman Jack spinning his tunes from a station that was incredibly far away. I wanted to wake up the entire family to experience this phenomenon – but it was way too late to bring attention to the fact that I was still awake. I simply covered my head in order to better hear the man and his music. It was indescribable excitement.

It became my routine to place the small radio under my pillow each night until I became sleepy enough to turn it off and place it on my nightstand. Sometimes I dozed off and ran down my batteries, or woke up early in the morning with the music still radiating from my pillow. My transistor radio was with me all the time, and I loved being able to listen no matter where I was. For me, it absolutely ignited my love for the new music that my older friends were listening to on the radio.

There were several technological innovations associated with the transistor radio. For the first time, radios could be turned on instantly without the need to wait for tubes to heat up before they were effective. I remember my grandfather (Pop) turning on his large, wooden, cabinet-model radio and waiting for several minutes before the sound came out of the speakers. With my transistor model, the instant you switched it on, sound was available. Power for the new radio was also new to the electronic world – the 9-volt battery was introduced to be used in transistor electronics. Finally, virtually all commercial broadcast receivers, pocket-sized or not, are now transistor-based.

I loved my pocket-sized radio more than any gadget that I had ever owned. I spent an enormous amount of time watching the shelves of the Western Auto Store to see if new models were available. When I was approximately 14, I saw something on the shelf that grabbed my attention. Sitting there in front of me was a new transistor radio that not only had AM channels but also had FM and Shortwave capabilities! It even had a leather case! And stereo earphones! The price tag was almost $100, and I wanted it badly.

At the time, I was riding around Mt. Vernon on my Schwinn Black Phantom bicycle. I had already started to drive Pop's automobiles so I was getting bored with my bike. I asked the owner of the store if he was interested in making a trade. He took my bike for a spin and when he returned he said he would trade the new radio even for my bicycle – if my mother agreed.

That night I explained the proposed deal to Bee, and she said the choice was mine to make. She did emphasize that the family would not be buying me another bike if I became dissatisfied with the trade. The next day I rode my bike to the Western Auto Store and came home with that new radio. I loved this model even more than I did my first. I even took it with me to UK after I graduated from high school.

I still have that radio fifty years later. And I wouldn't take the world for it. Okay, it's mostly for the sentiment of the role that it played in my young life, but it is also a small treasure from the still-developing world of electronics. And besides, I still love it.

T.V. icon The Lone Ranger

Hi-yo, Silver, Away!

A few days ago a new restaurant opened in Stanton, and my friend Hayden Johnson informed me that it would be offering cereal as one of the menu items for breakfast. He and I had formerly discussed that we both love a bowl of cereal with our morning coffee, so this was good news to me.

Our conversation reminded me of the countless times that my mother purchased a variety of cereal types for my approval when I was a very young boy. Of course, my choice was the cereal brand that contained the newest toy that came inside the box, or that could be purchased at a nominal price from the cereal company.

At that time in my youthful life, my favorite toys were small cars or anything that pertained to cowboys. I remember opening a box of General Mills Cheerios and finding an announcement that offered a Lone Ranger ring if you would send in the coupon and a small fee.

The ring was an ugly gold with a small "bump" on the top of it and a hole in each end. The cereal offer asked the consumer to send a photo of a child, and it would appear, when looking through the hole, that he or she was standing next to the Lone Ranger and Silver, his horse. I hounded my mother to send in the coupon with my picture, and finally she agreed to give me the money for the ring.

The ring arrived to my utter joy in just a few weeks! When I looked inside the hole on the ring, there I was standing next to the Lone Ranger and Silver. I showed it to all my friends and that silly plastic ring became one of my most prized possessions.

Because of my ring, the Lone Ranger also became one of my

especially favorite western heroes. I made a black mask out of an inner tube, and I painted my "stick horse" silver so that I could tame the West in our section of Rockcastle County.

My grandparents even bought me a Lone Ranger set of guns and holsters. I had about a dozen silver bullets on the back of my belt.

For those who do not remember, the Lone Ranger was an early television star. The usual opening announcement on the show was, *"A fiery horse with the speed of light… a cloud of dust… and a hearty 'Hi-yo, Silver, away!'"* The character was a Texas Ranger in the American Old West, who galloped about righting injustices with the aid of his clever, native Indian partner, Tonto. His horse, a beautiful white stallion, was called Silver.

The background story to the show was that a Texas Ranger had been wounded by outlaws, but he was found by an Apache Indian who nursed him back to health. Together they decided to form a team to fight crime and keep the identity of the Ranger a secret.

The Lone Ranger's use of only silver bullets was supposedly symbolic. The costly metal was to remind him that life, too, is priceless and, like his silver bullets, not to be wasted. During their adventures, Tonto often referred to the Ranger as "kemo sabe," a word meaning "faithful friend" in his tribe's language.

My neighborhood soon noticed that there was a new cowboy hero riding a silver stick horse who was there to protect them from "rustlers" and other bad men. And I was diligent in my pursuit of crime.

My mother had to ask me to remove my mask when it was time for dinner. My faithful silver stick horse waited patiently for me beside the kitchen door. I did not even have to tie him to the screen door; he was dedicated to assisting me in eliminating crime in our locality.

I slept with my guns and holsters. I was even known to put Silver under my bed on occasion in case I had to rush out to fight crime in the middle of the night. I even tied a red bandana around his neck to identify him from other silver stick horses.

The television episodes usually concluded with one of the characters lamenting the fact that they never learned the hero's name. Someone would say, "Who was that masked man?" – only to be told, "Why, he's the Lone Ranger!" The last new episode of the show aired on September 3, 1954.

The Lone Ranger continued to fight crime in comic books for many years after his final television show. I probably had every edition under my bed in a cardboard box. I read them over and over until I had them memorized.

Often I would take out my ring and wistfully stare at me and the Lone Ranger standing side by side. Then we would proceed to determine where we would fight crime this week. There were no bad guys hanging around my neighborhood – that masked man and I had it covered!

A Most Unusual Tree Fort

Climbing trees and building tree forts — as young boys, most of us loved to play in the woods for such adventures.

But there was one summer when we improvised and built our fort in a most unusual place: on top of my grandfather's outhouse! Before you begin to shudder at such an arrangement, a brief explanation is necessary.

Following the Great Depression, many outhouses were constructed for the benefit of rural families by a program called The Work Projects Administration. The WPA was created by President Franklin Delano Roosevelt in order to create jobs after the stock market crash of 1929. (Pop used to say in jest, "WPA means We Piddle Around.")

Those outhouses were extremely well constructed with concrete floors, sturdy walls, and well-built roofs. The privy at Pop's house was located on the side of his property near a gravel road that led to his garage and was in a place that gave us some privacy.

It was while Bee and I were living with Pop and Mommie Katie that my friends and I decided that the top of the outhouse would be a good place for us to build a fort.

We figured that, with such a sturdy rooftop, we could design a great temporary "clubhouse" so we could hide from our friends and also could see what was going on in the yard. The privy was located in the middle of three large locust trees, and the summer foliage offered lots of privacy.

Our design was pretty simple (remember, we were very young). We stretched a rope from one tree to the others and then hung blankets for the walls. We even nailed some wooden boards to one of the trees to serve as a ladder to get to the top of our secret hide-out.

Tree forts were great escapes for lying back, listening to the wind in the tree tops, and for watching wildlife in the area. The first day that we completed the final stages of our new project, we were sitting and looking around the tree tops when we spotted a bird nest filled with young birds.

For days on end we carefully watched the robins feeding their young. Because we were so close, it was a real education for boys who were only seven or eight years of age. The mother robin would bring whole earthworms to the nest and feed each baby a portion of the worm. We got a good laugh listening to the babies as they screeched for another piece.

There were several boys who lived in our neighborhood, and we decided that we would make our fort into a clubhouse with social gatherings for "members only." We settled on the requirements for membership and came up with the following list:
- Boys only (of course!)
- One member would serve as the Captain
- Dues would be 5 cents per week for each member
- We had to vote to see how the money was to be spent
- We also had a password to gain entrance to the fort—the secret word was "Robin."

Since the tree house was in a rather obscure location, we brought in a small, wooden, ammo box to hold our secret possessions so we would not have to carry them up the ladder each time we visited our fort. The box was kept locked, and the Captain was the holder of the key. Inside were a notepad and pencil, a pair of binoculars, a whistle, and a pocket knife. These were very important items to be in a tree house for boys of our age. My grandmother donated a large, slightly torn umbrella for us to use when it rained. We hung that umbrella on one of the tree limbs in case of emergencies.

One thing I can remember distinctly was my dog sitting at the base of the ladder nailed to the locust tree. His name was Frisky, and he could not understand why he was not allowed to enter our fort. Each day Frisky romped with us in the yard having as much fun as we were, only to be left alone at the bottom of the ladder when we climbed into our "secret hideout." After he died, I often thought of him sitting on the ground wishing he could join us on top of the privy.

One day, my friend Kenneth Hansel suggested that we gather as many extension cords as we could find and equip our fort with electricity. We all thought it was a great idea, so off to our respective homes we ran. If memory serves me right, we had to stretch 10 or 12 cords across the yard and up the tree to have lights at night. Can you imagine our neighbors seeing a lamp on top of Pop's outhouse when it got dark in the evening? I can hear them now, "What would possess anyone to have a light on top of a privy?"

In addition to the light, we also had a small electric radio on the roof of our hideout. We spent many nights sitting on that roof reading comic books while listening to the radio. We were totally entertained and happily content until we heard Mommie Katie yelling, "David Joe, it is time to come in now!" As soon as we heard that call, we gathered our personal belongings and down the ladder we went.

The only other detail that I can recollect about our fort is almost a cliché concerning young boys and their clubhouses — it was a sign nailed to the tree above the ladder which said "Do Not Enter – Members Only!" For a long time, that sign remained attached to the tree, even after we took down the ladder and stopped using the outhouse as a fort.

And that, my friends, is how you put a "fort" on top of a privy.

Pinball Wizard

Ever since I was a young boy
I've played the silver ball
From Soho down to Brighton
I must have played them all
But I ain't seen nothing like him
In any amusement hall
That ...kid
Sure played a mean pinball.
                                    The Who

The pinball machine and the jukebox were located in the back of the café. Teenagers gathered there to play their games and listen to the latest sounds. My parents operated the Ideal Café on Main Street in Mt. Vernon before I was even a gleam in my father's eye. It had been sold to Conard Parrot by the time I was in elementary school.

Youngsters lined up to play the pinball machine and competed with each other to see who could score the highest number of points. One fellow (his name escapes me) was truly a "pinball wizard," and he could beat any pinball machine in existence. Some of the business owners actually barred him from playing because the machines were no competition for his skills. He would run up hundreds of free games and give them to his friends. It cost a nickel to play. Some business owners even paid their customers for the "free" games they had won.

The jukebox always had the latest songs that were popular at the time. Six songs for a quarter was the price to listen to your favorite 45 rpm records. I still remember the grand Wurlitzer in the back of the Ideal Café with its cool sounds and flashing multi-colored lights. It was the focal point of the café.

Each week, we waited for the traveling "music man" to bring the latest hits to be placed on the jukebox. Sometimes he would give us the 45's that he removed from the machine. They would be scratched and worn but we were glad to take them anyway.

By the time we were in high school, our local hang-out was the Dinner Bell Restaurant. It, too, had a jukebox, and we fed it our quarters as we ate the hamburgers and fries and visited with our friends. The music never stopped! As soon as one of us ran out of quarters, someone else took over feeding the machine. We had to have our music. It was new and fresh, and we could not get enough of rock and roll.

According to my friends Hayden Johnson and Bud Parks, the local hangout for teenagers in Powell County was Dalton's Restaurant in Stanton. It was owned by Gilbert and Martha Dalton and served the best food in the area. The restaurant was also the location of the Greyhound Bus Station.

Dalton's, like the Ideal Café, was the place to listen to the Jukebox and play pinball machines. Teenagers made it their second home, sampling the great food and spending time with friends. Hayden said, "It never was an unruly place because Martha ran a tight ship." Almost any kind of food was available, and the reputation of the restaurant spread throughout the area. "People would come from several counties because of the reputation of the food and the atmosphere," Bud added.

In this day and age, youngsters have more sophisticated games and music players in their homes than we had in the cafés of the 50s. They simply turn on their iPods (20,000 songs) and grab their gameboys (multiple games) and entertain themselves for hours and hours. The digital format eliminates all the hiss, pops, and cracks of the music we enjoyed on our jukeboxes. The hand-held game players offer a wide variety of games including a new "pinball game" that resembles the large pinball machines that we used.

Even though I love the new technology of today, I still love running across cafés with the old pinball games and jukeboxes from days of old. Those truly "were the days!"

Making Shavings with Pop

Recently, I was looking through some of my old pocket knives (which I have collected for over 50 years) and found the one my grandfather gave me when I was a young child. Holding this worn and tattered Camillus Gran'pa, two-blade, pen knife took me back to the days when Pop and I would sit under one of the trees in his yard and whittle for hours on end. At first I was only allowed to watch – until he determined that I was old enough to own my first pocket knife. At that time, he drove me into town to visit Cox Hardware Store (still in business) on Main Street in Mt. Vernon. Pop told John Cox what he was looking for and we were shown my knife. "We'll take it," Pop said.

It is impossible to explain just how grown up and "manly" I felt having my own knife. I was only eight or nine years old. As soon as we got home, Pop gave me a lecture on the proper procedure to whittle safely as well as how to care for my shiny Camillus. I must have used an entire can of 3-in-1 oil during the first week. One of the safety procedures that he taught me about whittling was to always cut away from your body. He had learned that lesson the hard way. As a child, he had cut a large gash in his own leg by cutting toward his body. He showed me the scar to reinforce the lesson.

Stored in his chicken house were small pieces of cedar to be used only for whittling. He told me to take one piece at a time and to "use it up" before getting another. I remember well the wonderful times we shared and the smell of the wood shavings that would pile up on the grass between our legs as we whittled the afternoons away. His objectives were to make shavings and to produce a perfectly smooth piece of wood. When I asked him when we were going to make something, he replied, "We are making something – we are making shavings." I don't think he ever knew just how precious those hours together under a shade tree were to me.

When I turned 12, I returned to Cox Hardware and bought a knife by myself. It was a Boker Tree Brand with four blades. In those days, most knives were not stainless, so the oil was a necessary addition to your collection. From then until now, I am never without a trusty pocket knife.

Over the years, I have purchased, traded, and collected knives. When my son Todd was ten, I bought him his first, a Case XX. He seemed so proud of that knife, and I knew exactly how he felt. We sat on our patio, and I taught him the lessons that Pop had taught me.

This past weekend, I retrieved three knives that belonged to my son Todd before he died. Memories and intense feelings rushed through my mind as I held the knife that Pop had given me in one hand and the one I had given Todd in the other. The emotions see-sawed between joy and sorrow as tears filled my eyes. Both of those items are invaluable to me because of their history. I keep most of my knives in my lock-box, but ever so often I take out a different one to carry just to be able to touch something so closely connected to loved ones who are waiting on the other side.

Most of my collection actually consists of those that I purchased while on vacation in a special place or meant to remind me of a significant date. When I retired from teaching, my colleagues gave me a gift certificate to L.L. Bean, and I ordered a small pen knife to keep as a memento of that event. One of my most cherished is one given to me for Christmas two years ago by my wife. It is a Case canoe with handles of Mammoth Ivory that is 12,000 years old.

I consider it most unfortunate that whittling is seldom practiced anymore. In my day, one could always find several older gentlemen in the process in the yard of any local courthouse. They were as much a fixture as the benches themselves. Those men created a serene and peaceful atmosphere that somehow let you know – even as a child – that there was more to life than work and worry. Their pocket knives were tools to be used to help savor the quality of time well spent with friends, or family, or community.

Joyce Aylette and David Joe (1959)

Halloween Carnival

*D*on't you just love fall? I do, and each year at this time I am reminded of the Halloween Carnival which was held at Mt. Vernon High School (MVHS) when I was a teenager.

The MVHS annual Halloween Carnival was used to raise money for the school. Each classroom was transformed into an individual location for a part of the fall celebration, and patrons purchased tickets to enter the rooms. Games or booths filled all of the rooms. One room was assigned to adults from the county, who created a "spook house." It was very dark with people dressed in scary costumes. They would make you think that you could never get out without being tossed into a boiling cauldron of witches' brew. It was one of the best haunted houses that I ever experienced. (The emphasis was on fear; not grossing people out as is often done today.)

Another room was dedicated to a cake walk. (You remember those, don't you?) After selling tickets for the chairs, which were arranged in a circle, the music began. When it stopped, everyone had to find a seat. Each time someone was eliminated, another chair would be removed. The person claiming the final seat won the cake, which had been baked and donated by some good soul, usually a parent.

Other rooms contained duck ponds, a ring toss, and various games of chance. The lunchroom was the site of a minstrel show that highlighted talented locals who sang and played musical instruments. Some of the singers actually performed at Renfro Valley on the weekends. This artistic group always drew a large crowd, and it was the highlight of the evening.

Our gymnasium was the most unique and unusual of any basketball court that I have seen. It was in the basement of the school with the classrooms on the ground floor. The rooms opened onto a square and overlooked the gym in the center. Because seating on the gym floor was quite limited, spectators lined the halls to watch the games being played below. Many sat on the rail looking down into the gym. At carnival time, it became a showcase for the string of king and queen contestants who were paraded down a long runway to a throne which had been created on the stage.

The most memorable part of the carnival was the annual King and Queen contest. Each class in school elected king and queen (prince and princess) contestants to vie for the overall title of Halloween King and Queen. Jars and boxes to allow individuals to vote for the contestants were placed all over school and around town. Each vote cost a penny.

When I was a freshman, I was elected to represent my class as the king candidate and the class queen candidate was Joyce Aylette. Although my family was willing to donate to the cause, it never really occurred to me that Joyce and I might win.

To my extreme surprise, we were voted Halloween Carnival King and Queen. Joyce received her crown with the traditional scepter and a bouquet of long-stemmed roses and grinned with delight. As the crown was placed on my flat-topped head, I heard my father yell from the distant end of the gymnasium, "Kiss her, Joe!" The crowd roared. I was never so embarrassed in my life. (I didn't kiss her – at least not then.)

After the ceremony was over, we all went to Joyce's house and had a party. Her parents must have known that she was going to win because the party was obviously not one that had been thrown together at the last minute. We had a great time. (I might have kissed her then.) We actually dated until she moved to Texas at the end of our sophomore year.

Halloween will always remind me of the fun we had during the annual carnival. Good, clean, uncomplicated fun was the intent of the evening, and it remains in my mind just that way.

An old coal bucket

The Teen
Years

Kenneth Hansel

Friends Helping Friends

When I was a small boy living in Mt. Vernon, it was customary for us to help our friends with their chores so that we could go play when the work had been completed. Each of us had assigned jobs around the house, and we never gave it a second thought.

For example, when I was seven or eight years old, it was my responsibility to fill two coal buckets every evening after school, placing them behind the coal stove in the kitchen. Another chore of mine was to draw water out of our well, filling two buckets for the kitchen counter. And on a weekly basis, I had the task of cutting up small pieces of kindling and filling a wooden box so that my mother could start fires in the morning to cook breakfast. These duties were just part of being a member of the family. It was expected of young children of that day; it was good experience for them.

Now that I have reached my golden years, I sometimes ponder the chores my friends and I had, recounting the times when we helped each other get them done in order to spend our time having fun.

One of my first really good friends was Kenneth Hansel, who lived just across old US 25 from my house in the Pine Grove section of Rockcastle County. There were countless times when we assisted one another in order to complete our duties. As soon as we could, we were often heading for the woods.

One of Kenneth's obligations was to weed his family's vegetable garden, and their garden was quite large. I remember knocking on his door one fine Saturday morning to see if he could go to Big Fill cave with me. His mother informed me, "Kenneth has to hoe the garden before he can do anything else."

So of course we grabbed two hoes and ran into his garden. You never saw two little boys work so hard. In a couple of hours that garden patch was pristine. His mother came down and inspected our work. Finding the job satisfactorily performed, she released us, saying, "Now you can go play."

On numerous occasions Kenneth came to my house and helped me carry in coal or mow the lawn so that we could play in the woods behind my house. One particular day, my grandfather had already informed me that he needed my help picking corn for my grandmother, who would cut the corn off the ears and can it for later use. When Kenneth came over, we grabbed two galvanized buckets and headed straight for the garden. Within a short time, we returned with enough corn to keep Mommie Katie busy for several hours. We then immediately ran straight into those woods. To see us, someone might think there was a fire or something, but we were just being boys. Boys run.

As we grew older, the responsibilities remained, but the specific chores were changed – or added to. Jim Barton Nunnelley had a very substantial paper route, delivering the daily *Courier Journal* in Mt. Vernon on his Vespa moped. On evenings when I spent the night with Jim Barton, we had to be up at 4:00am in order to complete the delivery on time. While he drove, I sat on the back seat and threw the papers onto the porches of his customers. He often commented to me that his job was much easier when it was the two of us performing the deliveries.

And after reaching the age of being able to drive, I could always count on Bobby Joe Sweeney to help me with my car. When preparing for a double date, we worked together cleaning and waxing my '58 Chevy. Bobby did not have access to a car and loved to go with me. All I had to do was go by his house to pick him up, and we'd take my car to Pop's back yard and get out the hose. The two of us could make an automobile sparkle and shine.

One Saturday morning, I drove down to Gary Coffey's house to pick him up to play basketball at Jim Barton's basketball court. When I got there, he was busy raking leaves for his Dad. He asked if I could help him, already knowing that I would. We went to his garage, got the extra rake, and in short time all the leaves were gathered in bags for his father to haul off. We ran all the way to the basketball court.

Penny Nunnelley was a couple of years older than I was, but we occasionally double dated. Penny was responsible for running off the Sunday morning bulletin for the First Baptist Church, and I often helped him duplicate and fold the bulletins on Saturday afternoon so we could have plenty of time to get ready for our dates. We had loads of fun in that old Studebaker of his.

I even remember a girl helping me with a class assignment. When I was a freshman at Mt. Vernon High School, my English teacher gave the class an assignment of writing a poem to recite in class. I asked Nancy Helton to give me some ideas for my poem. The result was the only poem I ever wrote.

One of my friends was Charles Shivel and his sister was named Ruth Jane:

> *I looked up one street and down the other*
> *No one could I see but Ruth Jane's brother*
> *What I saw set my mind a whirl*
> *That bum was flirting with my best girl.*

When I read the poem to my English class everyone laughed and said it was very original. I don't think I ever thanked Nancy for her help.

I could not even begin to discuss how many times Buddy Cox helped me with my automobiles. And space certainly doesn't allow listing the specific times that he came to my rescue. He and I often worked on each other's cars. We habitually had great fun together – whether at work or at play.

In those days of the '50s and '60s, friends did not mind assisting each other with difficult chores. We did it because we were friends, and friends help each other. It was just that simple.

Pop's 1954 Chevy

Learning to Drive
and learning how not to drive

s mentioned before, my grandfather became the main male influence in my life when my mother and I moved in with him and my grandmother. I was very young at the time, and he made sure that he instructed me in the ways of becoming a man. He taught me how to drive a nail, shoot a gun, hunt, fish, and best of all – how to drive a car.

Upon listening to the Alan Jackson hit from a few years ago called "Drive For Daddy Gene," I was reminded of Pop's expert instruction. For the first time, the name "Daddy Gene" (or, in my case, Eugene) made me reflect on my own driving progress as a boy. The lyrics of the song caused me to pause and remember how it felt to drive for the first time.

> *It was just an old hand-me-down Ford*
> *With a three-speed on the column and a dent in the door*
> *A young boy – two hands on the wheel*
> *I can't replace the way it made me feel*
> *And I would press the clutch*
> *And I would keep it right*
> *And he'd say, "A little slower son, you're doing just fine."*
>
> *Just a dirt road with trash on each side*
> *But I was Mario Andretti*
> *When daddy let me drive.*

Pop instructed me about automobile safety when I was only ten years old by letting me sit on his lap and steer the family vehicle. When that was mastered to his satisfaction, he allowed me to sit under the wheel (he was sitting by my side) and actually drive the car on our gravel roads. Finally, when he was satisfied with my progress, he moved to the passenger side of the car and watched carefully as I developed my skills as a driver.

When I was about 14, he had established enough trust in me to let me take the family car and drive it throughout the neighborhood. The distance from our small farm to the Carter's farm was about two miles – and that became my route. At first, when I pulled out of our drive-way, he waited for me to return just to see if everything was alright. He consistently bragged on my skills and that gave me confidence. After a few weeks, he just pitched me the keys when I asked to drive to the Carter farm.

I don't have many regrets as far as Pop was concerned because I held him in very high esteem. He was, as I have said before, my hero. But there was this one day ...

A couple of my female friends had come to my house to listen to 45 rpm records. Their parents were to pick them up in a couple of hours. As all young boys, I thought it would be fun for the three of us to take a ride in Pop's '54 Chevy. He reluctantly said it would be alright if I took them on a ride to the Carter's house.

Sitting behind the wheel with two girls on board made my head swell and made my foot too heavy. I just had to show them how fast I could drive. As we passed into a curve on the gravel road, I lost enough control of the vehicle to bump a tree with the left rear fender. I was more concerned with Pop's confidence in me than I was with the condition of the car. It was only a slight dent. The girls were scared out of their wits. After calming them down, I took the car home and carefully put it inside Pop's garage.

The next morning, he backed the car out of the dark garage and drove to town to get the mail. When he came back home, he told me that someone had backed into his car and put a dent in it! I was riddled with guilt and heart-broken because I had not told him the truth about the wreck that I had caused the day before. And yet, I did not say a word.

I never did tell him the truth about the accident, and for over 50 years I have felt bad about not fessin' up. Pop lived to be almost 80 years old, and, to my shame, he died without knowing of my dirty little secret. I only wish I could look him in the eye and tell him how sorry I have been all these years for letting him down.

My '58!

Hubcaps and Whitewalls

When I began driving as a teen, it was important to me that my wheels and tires received the attention of my "hotrod" friends. The first automobile that I was able to drive by myself was a '54 Chevy, which was the family car. Without telling my grandfather, I secretly purchased a set of "baby moons" for covering the lug nuts of his car. To me, this addition set the car off, but Pop never noticed what I had done. I wanted to add a set of "porta-walls" but I knew that I couldn't get away with that because he hated white-wall tires.

I kept that old green and cream Chevy so clean that you could eat off the hood. It was the beginning of my obsession with driving clean automobiles. It remains with me today. I simply cannot stand to drive a dirty car. If I had all the money I have spent washing the cars that I have owned, I am sure that I could order a new Corvette.

The first car that I owned myself was a '58 Chevy. When I washed it the first time, the car was like a new canvas to an artist. It needed customizing badly. For some reason, I believed that the wheels needed to be the first thing modified. To accomplish this first stage, I purchased a set of "porta-walls" to give the appearance of having white-walled tires. After the installation, I stepped back and observed the change.

I determined that hubcaps were definitely needed to complete the look of the wheels. Into my bedroom I went to find my J.C. Whitney catalog. I flipped it open, and there in front of me was a set of chrome "flipper" hub caps, which I immediately ordered for my black Chevy. For the next two weeks, I patiently awaited the arrival of my package from the Whitney Company. When it finally arrived, I immediately removed the original Chevy caps and replaced them with my new "flippers." Now I was getting somewhere.

Because the '58 was my first car, it was my impression that I needed a second set of hubcaps – to give me the ability to modify the look of my car when I wanted to use it for special occasions. In those days, many young men opted for a set of '57 Plymouth spun-aluminum caps because they were relatively inexpensive and were easy to acquire.

I remember driving to Richmond to hunt for such a set at the junkyard located across from the Bluegrass Army Depot. The manager advised me to walk around the yard to see if I could locate a '57 Plymouth. He handed me a large screwdriver and said, "If you find what you are looking for, take them off and bring them to me."

After about an hour, I returned to the office and placed a set of spun-aluminum caps on the counter in front of the manager, who then quipped, "I am not going to charge you for the dirt that's covering these used hubcaps." I could hardly wait to get them home so that I could get out Pop's garden hose and clean those caps to a glimmering shine before installing them on my '58.

Over the next several years, I alternated the flippers and the spun-aluminum caps on my Chevy. When I wanted my vehicle to look really "cool," on went the flippers. When I desired a more distinguished look, I installed the spun aluminum caps. Needless to say, I thought my hubcaps and whitewalls looked splendid!

In 1963, I purchased my first new automobile, which was an Impala Super Sport Chevy. It was baby blue in color, had bucket seats, and four-in-the-floor. However, the hubcaps were stock, and I was not satisfied at all because the wheels did not have that young, customized look that I desired. Upon examination, my old flipper caps were too old and worn to be placed on my brand new vehicle.

So, guess what? Out came the J.C. Whitney catalog again. In a couple of weeks, my new flippers had arrived, and I immediately installed them on my new Impala. Once again, I was happy with the appearance of my wheels and tires.

When it came time to trade in my Chevy, I decided to purchase a new Pontiac. I was living in Campbellsville at the time and did my shopping at Beard Pontiac Oldsmobile. I ordered a new '68 Grand Prix Pontiac and spent the next several weeks waiting for its arrival. During those lingering days, I studied the brochure that displayed the hubcaps on my new Pontiac. I also carefully surveyed the hubcap section of my old Whitney catalog.

I finally came to the conclusion that I was now mature enough to be satisfied with the stock hubcaps that were already installed on my new car. Since that time in 1969, I have been content with the stock wheels and hubcaps that came with my new cars.

The fad of dressing up a car's wheels was great fun to me as a teenager. It was something that I loved to do with my automobiles because I believed that it gave my cars a more personal look. Now that I am a senior citizen, I merely update the wheels of a new car with chrome, increased-size wheels that can be added to the order. My current Ford Explorer has polished aluminum, 20-inch wheels that came with the vehicle.

I will always remember with great fondness the fun that I had customizing the wheels of my vehicles. I suppose it is because I spent so much time and attention on them that one of the first things that I notice on a car even today is its wheels. And, of course, I usually have an opinion about what, if anything, needs to be done with them to give that particular vehicle its best look. I suppose it's just ingrained in me – can I help it if I made myself an expert?

My Ford Explorer

My class ring
(Photo by Kelly Hobbs)

Class Rings Become Precious Mementoes

I became intrigued by class rings when I was just a small boy living with my mother in Mt. Vernon. One cold winter night, Bee decided to go through some of her high school and college memorabilia. We were sitting together by that wonderful Warm Morning stove in the living room of our small house. All of a sudden, she squealed with delight when she discovered the small box that held her class ring from Mt. Vernon High School (MVHS). She carefully removed it from its box, placing it on her right-hand ring finger. She held it out to me and said, "Isn't it pretty, David Joe?" I suppose a young boy could not forget seeing his mother so joyous.

I also recall when my brother Al was a junior in high school and received his class ring. He brought it home for me and Bee to see. They both spent a considerable amount of time discussing how great it was to have a souvenir of their days in high school. Since I was only six years old at that time, I was unable to fully understand just how important their rings were to them. But I got the general idea.

I even asked Bee if I could wear her gold ring for a little while, and she graciously granted my wish. I walked around with my finger extended and felt very important having a high school class ring on my small finger. After a short time, Bee said, "David Joe, give me back my ring so I can put it back in its proper container."

Class rings have had a long tradition. Apparently, it all began with the United States Military Academy, also known as *West Point*. It is the oldest military academy in the United States, having been established in 1802. In the year of 1835, the cadets began the tradition of wearing rings as a reflection of their unity, honoring their days at the academy. The custom has grown over the past 176 years, and now almost all schools and colleges have adopted and popularized the tradition.

In 1961, when I was a junior at Mt. Vernon High School, my class was called to the school cafeteria to hear a presentation about the purchase of our class rings by a representative of the Balfour Company. Up until that time, most class rings were oval in shape. Our class was given the opportunity to choose between the traditional oval shape or a new rectangular design. Samples of both were passed around for display, and then it was time to decide which design our class would order.

We voted and chose the new rectangle shape: a red stone with stripes of white mother of pearl. We thought our selection was the coolest ring we had ever seen. Later that year, our rings arrived. It must have been quite a scene as we all strutted around the halls of our school showing off our rings.

One of my good friends at MVHS, Lloyd Fain, was a year ahead of me in school, and I had already seen and admired his ring the year before. But there was a dramatic event that occurred involving his ring. He lived on a farm, and one day he was hulling corn to feed the hogs when his ring slipped off his finger. Only when he got back inside the house did he miss the ring. He searched and searched but to no avail. It had to have fallen into the hog lot!! Would you believe that later, almost exactly a year to the day, Lloyd's dad found that ring in that very location? It's true. (When I contacted Lloyd to make certain that my memory was correct about this, he was extremely surprised that I remembered this episode with his ring. We enjoyed a good chuckle about it.)

I also remember a particular evening involving my own ring. When I was a senior, I started to date a certain girl in my class. She was a cheerleader, so during basketball season she was wearing my ring. One night, in a hotly-contested basketball game, I noticed her actually pounding my ring against a metal fuse box that was located on a wall near the fans' section of the gym. I thought to myself, "She is going to ruin my ring!"

Sure enough, that night after the game, I asked to see my ring and to my utter dismay there was a chip on the corner of the red stone that formed the ring's design. I was not pleased. Now every time I look at my ring I remember how that chip was formed. Actually, I think the chip gives my ring a little extra "character."

As soon as I graduated from MVHS in 1962, I left Mt. Vernon immediately to attend summer school at the University of Kentucky. When I arrived on campus at UK, I already had plans to purchase a college ring as soon as I received my BS degree. Guess what? I have a ring in my jewelry drawer that shows my BS degree in science. When I earned my Master's degree from UK, my wife secretly purchased a MS ring from UK and presented it to me as a gift. I loved it, and I still wear that ring nearly every day.

In the summer of 1968, I began teaching chemistry and biology at Mt. Sterling High School and was also hired to be the assistant football coach. The following year, our football team won the Class A State Championship. That was one of the most exciting experiences that I ever had as a teacher – which is saying something since my career lasted for 38 years. A few years ago, I purchased a State Championship Ring as a memento of that sensational season. I would not part with it for the world.

I now have a total of four class rings, which I alternate wearing, and each one brings back wonderful memories of my past. I also still have my mother's high school ring in my collection.

High school and college class rings serve as powerful souvenirs of days long past. To most of us, they are real treasures. (I cannot imagine selling such rings for the cash they can bring!) I cherish each of my rings, and, on occasion, I pull them all out in order to reminisce about my life when I was younger. Each of them is a magical portal which opens into places, events, and friends from long ago.

Mt. Vernon High School

A Day at Mt. Vernon High

Living on the other side of the L&N Railroad from Mt. Vernon High School (MVHS) could be a stressful situation. This morning in December of 1961 is just an example. I woke up at daybreak, grabbed a bite of breakfast, and rushed out the door to get into my '58 Chevy in order to make my way to school. To my dismay, the front tire of my vehicle was flat, and I had to put on my spare. This distraction caused me to be late driving down US 150 toward school. Just as I rounded the corner of Main Street and Richmond Avenue, I noticed a train on the tracks in my path.

As I sat in my car waiting for the train to pass, I was thinking of how embarrassing it was going to be walking into home room tardy. Mrs. Lela Saylor was my homeroom teacher, and she did not allow any foolishness or tardiness. Sure enough, as I walked through the door, she asked, "Just where have you been, David Joe?" I told her my story, but as I explained each part (flat tire and a train delay), she seemed to question my truthfulness -- and so did my fellow classmates. "Go to the office and get a tardy note," she instructed.

After getting my tardy note, I was then late to my first period geometry class, which was taught by Assistant Principal Bill Landrum. He, too, questioned my timing. Would this day ever get back to normal? Several of my friends were in that class, so naturally they teased me for having such reasons for being late. Charles Shivel wanted to know if I had been out too late with one of my girlfriends the night before and asked, "Did you have a hard time getting home last night?" Marion Whitehouse, Lee Childress, Wayne Ballinger, and Dwight McNew joined in with Charles and poked fun at me for the rest of the class. Finally, the bell rang and into the hall we poured.

As I walked down the hall in order to visit my locker, I noticed Joe Lambert with another huge load of books under his arm. (Looking back at that day, he must have already been preparing to become the Chief Justice of the Kentucky Supreme Court.) While standing at my locker, Marty Sowder came up and asked, "Are you going skating in Berea on Friday night?" I responded by saying yes, and she reminded me that she would love to ride with me if that was alright. I was glad she asked because she was always fun to be with on the weekends. Even though she was a senior, we spent a lot of time together as friends and good buddies.

My next class was Chemistry, taught by Mr. Charles "Tuck" Baker. He began the class by giving us a quiz on the symbols of the elements listed on the periodic table. On the wall, above his head, was a very large Periodic Chart, but I am sure he did not remember that it was in front of us. For that particular quiz, we all made a perfect score. When the bell rang for us to go to our ten-minute break, we filed out of the door laughing at his mistake. Carla Baker, Sandy Murrell, Sharon Owens, James Cope, Lee Price and I laughed all the way to the soft drink machines. In a matter of a few minutes, everyone had heard about our good fortune. And yet, Mr. Baker never did realize that we were looking at the answers while taking that quiz.

After purchasing our soft drinks, most of the guys took a seat on the rail outside the boy's bathroom in order to listen to one of our favorite adults, Custodian Charlie Hines. All of the students loved him, and he was most proficient at his task of keeping our classrooms amazingly clean.

The next thing: lunch. MVHS had what is known as an "open" lunch period, meaning that students were permitted to leave campus to pick up something to eat. Bob Ford's Grocery was within walking distance from the school. Several of us decided to grab a slice of bologna on crackers for our meal that day. Marty Sowder, Bud Cox, Paul Daily, Nancy Helton, and I grabbed our coats out of our lockers and briskly walked across the street to purchase our lunch.

As usual, we had to stand in line to be served at the meat counter. I took my time getting back to class because I had Health and Physical Education under Coach Jack Laswell as my next class. He was not so strict about us being tardy, and we usually stretched our lunch period as long as we possibly could. When I arrived at the gym, the guys had already started to play basketball, so I quickly put on my Converse All-Stars and joined the game. Coach Laswell never knew I was late.

Following lunch and while on my way to the gym, I entered the school just in time to see the cheerleaders headed to the gym in order to prepare for a pep rally that was going to be held during the final portion of last period. There they were – all together – looking........ very fine. The group included: Nancy Helton, Carla Baker, Sharon Owens, Martha Sowder, Jewell Anderkin, and Dorcas Woodall. They were one noisy unit moving down the hall, gearing up for the rally and the game.

The last period of the day, I was assigned to a study hall which was conducted by Mrs. Doris Niceley. As I walked through the door, Charlotte Fain was yelling at me to come over to her table. I took a seat and chatted most of the period with her, Mary Daily, Jim Barton Nunnelley, and Lloyd Fain.

Lloyd and I decided to drive over to Berea that night to see what was going on at the local drive-in restaurant. Paul Daily came by later that period, and we asked him to go with us to Berea. During the last part of the period, we were called to the gym to join the pep rally to get us pumped up for a home basketball game that evening.

Finally, the closing bell rang, and we all casually walked out to the parking lot and filled our cars with teenagers. It was our custom to grab a snack at the Dinner Bell Restaurant at the end of the day. We ordered cherry Cokes and potato chips, which we dipped in ketchup. In the background, The Platters could be heard singing *The Great Pretender* on the jukebox.

1961 was a very good year!

The Little World's Fair

When I was a little boy, it was a yearly event for my Dad to put me into his pickup truck and head for the "Little World's Fair" in Brodhead, Kentucky. Occasionally, he allowed me to take along a friend. Because of the enormous crowds, we had to park about a mile away and walk to the fairgrounds. Daddy always complained about the heat and about the long walk to the day's events.

We usually spent some time at the horse show before venturing into the throngs of people who were purchasing tickets to board the joy rides. Daddy was not interested in riding himself, but he always allowed me to choose which rides I wanted to enjoy. He stood close by, watching me have fun.

Daddy was a "people person" and spent a great deal of time chatting with his friends. Everyone knew him and wanted to talk. Sometimes I became aggravated when he spent too much time chatting with his "buddies" instead of walking me through the ride area. I remember one year when Daddy actually rode the Merry-Go-Round with me. It was a real thrill to have him by my side. I was probably six or seven at the time. I don't recall that he ever did that again.

Part of our tradition was to sample most of the food items that were available at the fair. Daddy loved pork bar-b-que and usually tried to find a vendor that was serving good pork.

After lunch we had to find an ice cream stand to cool us off. In the afternoon, a variety of candy and fruit was the standard fare. I remember sitting under a shade tree while we consumed an entire watermelon. We had the sweet juice all over us by the time it was finished.

One of my favorite parts of the yearly event was the games of chance that had booths around the circle. As a very small child, I loved choosing the floating ducks to see which prize I could win. As I got older, winning a prize was much harder because the games of chance became more difficult to conquer.

As Daddy and I walked around the circle, fair workers barked at the crowd, trying to convince us to spend our money at their individual booths. One year Daddy got into a shouting match with a "pushy" carnival guy who wanted me to toss rings over Coke bottles.

Daddy threatened to "call the law" if he did not leave us alone. I am amazed that he did not pull his .38 special on the guy. (He carried his Smith and Wesson everywhere he went!) Daddy was capable of doing that if he was aggravated. I had seen him pull that trick before.

I distinctly remember one year when Daddy gave me a roll of quarters to play the games of chance. (A small fortune at that time!) He told me that he would be "right back." I was about 10 at the time. I saw him walking down to the tents at the back end of the carnival, and even then, I had a fairly good idea of where he was going—but of course I did not say a word. He returned about 30 minutes later. We never discussed where he had gone.

After I was old enough to drive, my trips to the fair involved taking a date instead of going with my dad. This was a totally new experience! Every girl that I ever met wanted her guy to win her a "teddy bear" to take home as a souvenir.

Because I wanted to please my date, my goal was to win the largest bear in the entire complex. Most of the time, it took several rolls of quarters to accomplish that feat. And, frankly, I was willing to spend a fortune.

There was one special date. Her name was Sandy Proctor. She wanted to see the horse show and even took a picnic basket for us to enjoy for lunch. After the horse show, we moved to a shady area and shared fried chicken, deviled eggs, and one of the best platters of fried apple pies that I had ever eaten. Not only was she exceptionally cute, but she could cook as well!

That evening we walked around the midway, indulging in every ride that she wanted. I even managed to win her a large, white Teddy Bear. I think I was Sandy's hero that day – or at least I certainly felt like I was!

Skating – On A Roll Again

*I*t was a Thursday at Mt. Vernon High School, and several of my friends had already asked if they could ride to the skating rink that night. Every Thursday and Friday nights in the early 60s, the fad was to visit the rink and skate the night away. We stayed as long as we could -- until midnight. The site of this party was in Berea, and we made the trip about twice a week for several years. The memory of this event is etched into my mind.

It was 18 miles from Mt. Vernon to Berea, and sometimes my '58 Chevy would have 10 or 12 teenagers piled inside to make the journey to the rink. The ride was almost as much fun as the actual party. We would sing along with Ray Charles as he sang, "Hit the Road Jack" or Dion's "Run-around Sue," as well as many other songs played on the Top 40 radio stations.

The rink was brand new and had a sound system that was state of the art for its time in 1960. Large speakers hung from the center of the dance floor. Mood lighting circled the floor. A disk jockey played hit records. The owner was a skate instructor, and he stayed in the middle of the circle to give free instructions to new members. This was a rink that required a membership. I think the fee was $25 per year. You could not simply walk up to the window and pay for one night's admission.

On Thursday nights, we all skated and practiced our skills for Friday night -- date night. Sometimes we also went on Monday evening to receive instructions on skate-dancing. Most of us could fast dance or waltz and manage to stay in rhythm. Some of us could actually skate backward as we faced our partners. If you could do that, all of the girls wanted to skate with you. (I quickly learned how.) Another large part of the Thursday session was consumed with guys wanting to skate fast and also to form fast Congo lines. If one of the leaders fell, then the entire group stacked up in a domino pile. It kept us in very good shape.

Friday nights were so cool. The DJ played a slow song after three "jitter-bug" tunes. At 11:00pm, all songs were for slow dancing until the place closed at midnight.

Located on one end of the rink was a very nice snack bar, which had several booths and tables. They sold great hamburgers and hot dogs. You could also get desserts and refreshing ice cream. When I was a senior, they added pizza to their menu. Before that time, the only pizza available came from Momma Mia's Pizza restaurant, but that is another story.

The big annual event was a Queen contest for the ladies. They were judged for their ability to dance on skates in addition to how cute they were. One year my first cousin asked me to be her partner. I'm glad to report that she won the contest in spite of my dancing skills. I still remember the large photo of Patsy which was hung in the lobby of the rink commemorating her victory.

The simplicity of that time was wonderful. All week long, we looked forward to the weekend gathering. Dates for Friday night were booked well in advance. The guys wore their best jeans and turned-up collar shirts. The girls usually wore sweaters and full skirts. It really was a lot like the sitcom "Happy Days" on television.

On date nights, we double dated so two couples could ride together. My best friend, Bud, was a very good skater and he rode with me. Where did those times go?

By the way, it seems that roller rinks are making a come-back! The list of events has also expanded. Today's rinks offer something for almost everyone: speed skating, artistic skating, roller fitness, specific music nights, and a thriving birthday party scene. You really should check out a rink in your area – you might make some memories of your own.

Patsy Cummins

My 1963 Chevrolet Impala Super Sport

My Chevrolet

Some time ago, my wife and I had an opportunity to attend the Grand Ole Opry in historic Nashville, Tennessee. It was our first experience with the live country phenomenon which began as a simple radio broadcast in 1925. We came away with Phil Vassar's name circled on our programme.

The Opry has been called the "home of American music" and the "country's most famous stage." It is dedicated to honoring country music's rich history and the present chart-toppers who are following in their footsteps. The night that we were in the audience, country music legend Charlie Daniels was the highlight entertainer.

Phil Vassar also performed that night and included the title song from his CD called, "Prayer of a Common Man." My wife liked the song so much that we purchased the CD almost immediately upon our return from Nashville. It's a good disc, but I was thrilled to find that it also contained an unexpected "gold nugget" of a song.

My favorite song from Vassar's CD is called "My Chevrolet." The moment I first heard it, I was transported back to 1963 and my own new Chevrolet. It was my first new automobile, and I had never been as excited. As soon as I drove it into Mt. Vernon, I headed straight to my friend Buddy Cox. Upon my arrival, he immediately insisted, "Slide over and let me drive!" It was my pleasure.

Of course, I took many of my friends for a ride in that Chevy, both later that day and for weeks and months thereafter. I was so proud. We had great fun tooling around in that car. Day or night, weekdays or weekends, whether an adventure or just a moonlit drive, that Chevy was my "magic carpet." Vassar's song captures it all:

I had a 327 and a 4 on the floor
It was Detroit built back in 1964 ('63 for mine)
Red bucket seats, she was all mine, all mine (mine were
   blue)
Yeah, was one of a kind
Kevin called "shot gun" and the boys piled in
We were young and we were innocent, we were guilty as sin
And every Friday night, we'd make our getaway
In my Chevrolet.

I will never forget the Friday nights that my friends and I spent driving that '63 Chevy all over Rockcastle County. We spent most of our time on back country roads, and Vassar's lyrics reflect those special nights:

Big, yellow moon on a country road
And "Night Moves" on the stereo
The windows down and the smell of fresh cut hay, hey, hey
If that Chevy could talk, the stories she'd tell
About broken hearts and love and raising hell.
Yeah, it was summertime
Man those were the days
In my Chevrolet.

Vassar could have been one of the boys in the backseat of my Chevrolet in those days because he relates the nights of fun we had parking, going to the Valley View Drive-In, and spending time at the Mt. Vernon water reservoir. Does this verse bring back memories for you?

Now, Jenni was an angel, she was my first love
Steaming up the windows and getting all tangled up
Stumbling around in the darkness and trying to find our
way, hey, hey
At the drive-in movies, parked way up in the back
I couldn't tell you what was playing, I didn't care nothing
about that

But after the show, we'd hit the road and park down by the lake
In my Chevrolet.

Those days seem so far in the past now that I have, for all practical purposes, reached the official stage of being labeled an "elderly person." Just today, a friend of mine asked, "Where did the time go?" I have no answer.

In many ways it seems like only yesterday that I was pulling up into the driveway of Cox Funeral Home to let Bud see my new '63 Chevrolet. Apparently, I'm not the only one who looks back with such fondness on those days because Phil Vassar's song echoes that time perfectly. And, unlike me, he is writing for the masses.

My '63 Chevy

My First Pizza Pie

O ne of my favorite hangouts as a teenager was a spot called "Little Mama's," which served something listed on the menu as "pizza pie." Little did I know that this new dish would become one of my preferred adult meals.

When I was young, there were no fast food restaurants in Mt Vernon. The only restaurants that we patronized were those with sit-down service and juke boxes at each table. The first true "fast food" that I remember was McDonald's in Lexington, and I was probably 12 years old before I sampled the cuisine at the Golden Arches.

In those days, the variety of trendy food was limited to good ole hamburgers and fries that local restaurants served. Shops such as Arby's, Wendy's, and DQ had not yet come upon the scene. Our beloved hangout was called the Dinner Bell, and all of the young people gathered there for food and fellowship. On Friday and Saturday nights, the place was full of guys and gals with their dates. Cherry Cokes with potato chips dipped in ketchup was the fad of the day.

When I reached the ripe old age of 16 and started to drive, several of us traveled the 18 miles up US 25 to Berea in order to check out the "college" bill of fare. One weekend, we noticed a restaurant on the back side of Boone Tavern called "Little Mama's." The owner was actually German and served something brand new to us – pizza pie.

Bertha Fish was the owner's name, but everyone called her Frau. Understand that this was my first time to taste this unique dish. The only pies that I had ever encountered were for dessert. This new chow was filled with meat, tomato sauce, spices, and cheese covering a thin pie crust. It was something very unusual for boys from Rockcastle County. We were hooked! From that point on, droves of teenagers piled into our cars and spent our weekend nights with "Little Mama."

It was an impressive date when we took our girlfriends to our newly found night spot. We wore our best Levis, white dress shirts (with the collar turned up), white socks, and Bass penny loafers. We strolled into Mama's and immediately loaded the juke box with coins. We listened to our favorite rock and roll songs while dining on pizza and Cokes. The place was always filled with students from Berea College as well as local high school students. There was a small spot for dancing if you gathered up enough courage. The girls always pushed us onto the dance floor – whether we wanted to or not.

The food at "Little Mama's" was simply outstanding. We were not accustomed to real Italian food, and we could not get our fill. The place became so popular that on Saturday nights you had to get there very early or very late. We kept the road hot between Mt. Vernon and Berea. (Remember, you could not order pizza for delivery.)

On nights when we were financially strapped, we ordered her awesome bread sticks and that fabulous garlic butter. All of this was completely novel to us at the time. Because we had discovered the place, we considered it ours. We had found a spot that was fresh and contemporary. What else could we need: pizza pie, Cokes, music, and "Little Mama" to watch over us?

Of course Little Mama's ceased to be years ago. I was broken-hearted when I learned that it was gone. (Just one more example of how so many things have changed over the past fifty years.) Maybe we could organize a "Little Mama's" reunion....

1960 Chevy Impala

Life at the Lebanon House

By the beginning of my junior year in college, I was living in an old house that had been converted to a residence for male students. The house, owned by a preacher, had been remodeled to accommodate 13 guys. We referred to our landlord as "The Reverend Mr. Black" because he actually was a minister and his last name was Black. The residence hall was known as The Lebanon House.

I fondly remember several other residents who shared the house with me. One of the most memorable was a guy we called "Sarge." He had served in Vietnam where he had lost his right leg from the knee down as a result of a land mine. Artificial limbs were not as sophisticated then as they are today and his was made of wood.

Sarge was a great guy with a wonderful and witty personality. All of the guys just loved the fellow, and he was fully one of us. As a result, we did not view him as "disabled," and we felt free to make him the brunt of our jokes out of our deep affection for him – just like we did with everyone else.

When Sarge was asleep, it was just too tempting for college boys not to steal his wooden leg. After all, it was just sitting there, waiting for adventure. We hid it in a variety of places around the Lebanon House. Sarge eventually started keeping a broom under his bed so that he could motivate around the house to search for it. Once we actually put it on the roof! Sarge took it all in fun with a most positive attitude and that made us love him even more.

Another personal friend of mine who lived in the Lebanon House was Delvin. He owned a hot 1960 Impala Chevy with a 348 cubic inch V-8 engine with a single Edelbrock 4-barrel carb. He thought it was "bad." At the time, I drove a 1963 Impala with a 327 V-8 engine. Mine had a four-speed "tranny," and his was a three speed on the column.

On several occasions, we paired them up for the quarter mile competition. Sometimes he would win by a very short margin, and other times the race would be mine. Delvin could not let it go!

One night about 2:00am, he came charging into my room and challenged me to one last quarter-mile contest. Of course, the drag strip was closed at that time of the night, so we lined them up on Lebanon Avenue right in front of the house. Two of our friends assisted in the contest. One started the race; the other was a quarter mile up the street waiting for us to finish.

And once again, it was just too close to call! Delvin and I both spent the rest of the evening (or should I say morning) claiming victory over the other. Because of the noise, we were afraid to give it a second run. (Neither one of us wanted to be lodged in the county jail for racing on a city street.)

Actually, I was glad when it finally ended. A few weeks later, Delvin graduated. There never was an official determination of which of us had the "badest ride."

Other memories from life at The Lebanon House also come to mind. One night we were watching UK basketball on television. The Cats were in a mighty battle with the Tennessee Vols. At the last moment, a guard hit a jump shot from almost mid-stripe to beat the Cats – and only a split second later, one of the guys threw a Coke bottle from across the room through the black-and-white TV screen.

Sparks and fire flew all over the room. And the smell – just horrible! We were scared out of our wits. I never saw that many guys get into bed as fast in my life. When asked what happened the next day, everyone simply replied, "What game?"

One of the funniest memories that I have is one night when one of the guys was in the bathroom. He was sitting on the commode reading a magazine when the throne "settled" about six inches into the floor. Upon hearing the noise, we all ran into the bathroom to see what was going on.

The view was priceless. There he was, still sitting on the throne but with his knees practically even with his chin. Water was spraying all over the room, and the expression on his face was like something out of a comic strip. We laughed until we cried.

Life at the Lebanon House was truly an unforgettable experience.

The Tale of the
Watermelon Truck

Okay, I admit it. I was a thief – but dad-gum-it, it was fun. As teenagers, we just didn't consider stealing watermelons a crime; we just thought of it as a silly prank. It takes looking back on the adventure from a considerable distance to realize that it actually was a crime – one for which we could have been seriously punished.

The night to which I am referring occurred when I was sixteen years of age and had just begun to drive. Several of my friends and I were sitting on the side of the street in Mt. Vernon when we noticed a large semi hauling a load of watermelons down Richmond Street toward Renfro Valley. (Remember, there was no interstate at this time.)

Someone said, "Let's head off the truck on Greenfish Hill!" So, we did. We piled into my car and raced toward Renfro Valley in order to beat the truck to the mile-long hill on the other side of the valley.

We gathered speed to the top of the hill and parked. The guys and I jumped out of the car and ran back down the hill to hide in a ditch beside the road. Our plan was to meet the truck filled with the melons before it reached the half-way point up the rise.

When it did, a couple of guys jumped onto the back of the trailer and began to toss off watermelons to those of us running on the road behind the truck. We carefully laid them on the side of the road and came back for more.

Keep in mind that the truck probably contained several hundred melons, and we only took what we could put in the trunk of my '58 Chevy. The total number of melons most likely numbered a dozen or so.

As soon as we thought we had enough, the guys jumped back

onto the highway, and we watched the semi creeping into the distance on its way to the top of the hill toward Berea. We immediately hiked back to my car and drove down the hill to retrieve our "bounty." We carefully filled my trunk and headed back to Mt. Vernon to display our prizes to our friends (and girlfriends) waiting on Main Street.

Someone suggested that we share our wealth with any teenager in town that night. In order to do so, we went into the Dinner Bell Restaurant and borrowed a large kitchen knife to slice the melons. Before long, teens up and down the street were consuming the ripe, sweet melons and were coming back for more.

In our minds, we were heroes because we shared our prize with anyone who wanted a sample. We laughed for days afterward as we remembered the prank that we had pulled off.

One of my teachers got wind of the theft, and she reminded me of how disappointed my mother would be if she heard about my involvement in this escapade. That got me to thinking!

If my mother had actually found out what we had done, she would have skinned me alive. And I am sure that she would have locked up my car for a month or even longer. Bee would never have understood the fun of stealing *anything*. Remember, this is a woman who read the Bible from cover to cover twenty-three times.

Because Mt. Vernon was such a small town and everyone knew everyone else, I sweated for several weeks hoping that no adult would hear of my offense and tell Bee. It turned out that I was just plain lucky. She never did find out about my "dastardly deed," and I was so relieved.

Some might wonder why I have not included the names of my co-conspirators. To be perfectly honest, I don't remember precisely who they were. And honestly, I am as curious as anyone as to their identities. If you were with me on that fateful night, please drop me a note or e-mail and "fess up!"

By the way, I still love watermelons, don't you?

Buddy Cox and Dave Griffin

Travelin' with Bud

The year was 1961. At sixteen years old and with a car of my own, I was itching to take a trip for spring break – something that high school kids rarely did in those days. But how to convince my mother to allow me to do so? I had my best ally in my friend Buddy Cox – who was a whole year older and had training and experience as an ambulance driver.

We decided our best shot would be a trip to Washington, DC. At that time, my brother Al and his wife lived in Manassas, Virginia – only 40 miles from DC. We called and confirmed that they would be glad to have visitors from home. Although somewhat apprehensive, my mother apparently trusted that we were responsible enough to make the trip.

This was about the same time that I had "customized" my '58 Chevy; so obviously we would drive it to Washington. I had always been very picky about who could drive my car (I still am), but Buddy had driven on our double dates many times. Therefore, we decided to take turns and to drive "straight through" to Manassas.

My grandmother volunteered to prepare a picnic basket for us to take along. She fried chicken, baked rolls, and topped it off with a surprise loaf of her much loved banana-nut bread. I think she intended the treats to last for a good portion of the trip; however, the aroma of that loaf was too much for Bud and me. As soon as we pulled out of the drive-way, we grabbed the banana-nut loaf, simply broke it in half, and started to chow down. It was gone before we crossed the Rockcastle River on the other side of Livingston. Growing boys need nourishment, so the chicken and rolls were also history by the time that we reached Corbin.

It is important to note that there were no interstate roads. From Mt. Vernon to Al's house, we had to wind our way through the mountains of Virginia. It was actually fun because we were able to visit many small towns and see lots of new places on our adventure.

One of the remarkable places that we visited was Shenandoah National Park as we drove up the Blue Ridge Parkway, a rural scenic highway. My brother had advised us to get off on Skyline Drive to see the wildlife, and we loved that part of our trip. Deer and other small animals were spotted around nearly every turn.

Late at night, while still in the mountains of Virginia, a cold rain began to fall. It was so cold that it started to freeze on our car. Riding in the passenger seat, Buddy told me to take a look at the radio antenna. The freezing rain had built up on it until it was about the circumference of a half-dollar. We had to stop and physically break the ice off the front of the car. It was exciting stuff for two high school boys on an adventure away from home.

The parkway ends near Front Royal, Virginia, and it was just a few miles to Manassas from that point. I had been to my brother's before, so it was easy to find his house. When we arrived the following morning, Eva had prepared a nice breakfast for the two of us. Al had arranged for some of the teenagers in his church to show us around Manassas. During the next few days, we became acquainted with a lot of young people. They escorted us to local parties, pizza parlors, and bowling alleys. We had a big time.

Al and Eva showed us all the historic sites of Washington, D.C. The most memorable was the Washington Monument, the largest masonry structure in the world. We walked up the 897 steps and viewed all of Washington from this picturesque viewpoint. While at the top, Buddy noticed a small crack in the marble wall just above our heads. We scratched our initials on a penny and placed it in the crack. Throughout the following years, each of us has visited the monument on different occasions and found the penny remaining in its secret hiding place. However, the last time one of us checked was in 1997. Buddy was there and looked for our marker, only to find the area covered with plastic. Of course, we have chosen to believe that it will remain there for eternity.

After an enjoyable week, Buddy and I started our return to Mt. Vernon. We listened to rock and roll all the way back, singing along with Ray, Buddy, Ricky, Dion, and Elvis. Since that time I have visited many areas of the country but this first adventure will remain one of my most memorable trips ever. And special thanks to Bud for his friendship for over 50 years.

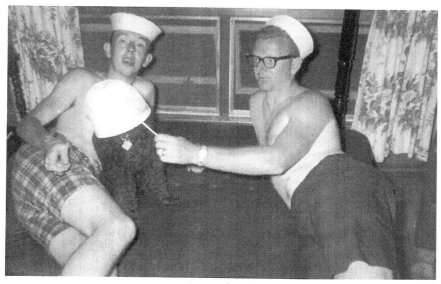

Me and Bud

Cruisin'

My 1958 Chevrolet

Black Beauty

I have always had a love for automobiles. When I was ten years old, my grandfather (the man I admired most in the world) decided it was time for me to learn to drive. He would take his 1954 Chevrolet Bel-Air out on a country road in Rockcastle County and, with me sitting closely by his side, he would let me steer. He told me to watch everything, including the rear-view mirrors, and to keep the steering wheel as steady as possible. After a couple of years of instruction, he moved to the passenger side and let me drive.

Of course, this was a manual shift automobile, and I was taught to shift very carefully so that the passengers would not feel the car jerk. By the time I was 14, he was allowing me to drive the car by myself on gravel roads on our farm and occasionally up to a little country store to fetch groceries. This training was, as you might expect, very exciting to a teenager, and I looked forward to his instructions concerning the family car.

When I turned 16, Pop helped me to purchase my own car. It was a black 1958 Chevrolet that was my whole world. I began immediately to customize it. First, I took it to a local body shop and made a deal with the owner. He agreed to work on my car, and I would help him at his shop. We took off all of the chrome, leaded in the holes, and repainted it jet black. Next we put chrome accessories on the engine and purchased "flipper" hubcaps for the wheels. We also lowered my car about four inches so it would have the look that was in vogue at the time. Finally, I had an upholstery shop "roll and pleat" the interior. I was the proudest 16-year-old in Rockcastle County.

I faithfully washed my car at least twice a week and changed the oil every 1500 miles. The customary pair of dice hung from the rearview mirror. The last expense that I remember was driving my car to Lexington to have a custom radio installed, including a rear speaker with a fader switch.

Some of my favorite memories revolve around this first automobile of mine. When I am with friends from my high school days, they tell me stories about that car. It seems that each one of them has a different memory of some event – but they always remind me that we were in the '58 Chevy. A dear friend (Martha) recently said she remembered us having 13 or 14 teenagers riding around town listening to our music. That was common for us to spend time that way – singing to the top of our voices as we listened to rock and roll! Driving and singing the night away together.

No one was ever more proud of his car than I was, and a couple of years later I took it to the University of Kentucky with me – even though freshmen were not permitted to have cars. I found an elderly couple who lived close to campus who let me park in their driveway for $5.00 a month. I was only supposed to use the car on the weekends and use it I did. I visited every drive-in that was even remotely close to Lexington.

Multiple decades later, my love for 1958 Chevrolet automobiles still remains. If I ever hit the lottery, my desire is to locate a model exactly like my "black beauty" and restore it to its former glory.

Lloyd Fain, Bud Cox, and Marty Cox

Me and Jerry Hansel

Boys and their Cars

*I*n the early 60s, young men took care of their own cars and took a great deal of pride in knowing how to make basic repairs. We learned these skills from our parents, grandparents, brothers, and especially other friends.

"Back in the day," it was necessary to make many of our own restorations because we did not have the cash to pay someone to do the work for us. My friend Buddy Cox explained, "I learned a lot about basic car repair from my brother Billy; he learned from Dad, and Dad received a lot of his knowledge from his father. It was common for us to replace points and sparkplugs, tune up our engines, and even do more difficult repairs. I replaced a head gasket on a '31 Model A Ford Deluxe Coupe, which I owned at the time."

It was interesting to discuss this subject with Bud because I learned a lot about general automobile repair from him, from Charles Hensley, and from my grandfather. I remember one Saturday afternoon when Bud and I changed the plugs and points on my '58 Chevy. We simply pulled my car under a shade tree behind Cox Funeral Home, raised the hood, got out our tools and started to work. In those days, completing a general tune-up was a simple matter.

The job was finished in approximately 45 minutes. We did not have to deal with computers, high-priced electronic testing equipment, or complicated automobile parts. One of my Stanton, Kentucky friends recently said, "Today, cars are so complex that you have to take off the entire front end to replace a headlight, and it costs $350!" I can remember having a line drawn on the Standard Oil Station inside wall in Mt. Vernon that gave you the ability to correctly aim a new headlight so it would be in the proper alignment. By the way, a headlight in those days cost about $3 each.

I remember another time when Charles Hensley and I replaced the clutch and pressure plate on my '58 Chevy late one night at Baker's Standard Oil after the place had closed. Charles worked for Baker and had a key. That afternoon he sent me to the parts house to get the necessary items, and in a few hours I was "shifting gears" just like the car was brand new. Charles had a gift for automobile repair, and I learned many tricks from him.

He also assisted me with customizing the engine on that old black Chevy. We replaced the breather with one that was smaller and chrome-plated, installed new plug wires, replaced the manifold with one that was "split," and even put plugs in my manifold pipes so the car sounded like a souped-up V-8 engine. It was a thrill to take off those manifold caps and roar up US 25 making so much noise that everyone in the neighborhood would hear. With the assistance of Charles, Bud, and Pop, I put over 150,000 miles on that old Chevy, and I loved every mile that was registered on the odometer.

I also put a rear speaker and fader switch on the AM radio of my car and was so excited with the sound coming out of the dash and the back window area of my car. Rock and roll music never sounded so good! I had to run the speaker wires under the carpet with a coat hanger to make the connections. You never saw teenagers so excited as when we tuned in WAKY radio. We drove around for days listening to Buddy Holly, Ray Charles, Elvis, Roy Orbison, Ricky Nelson, and many other stars of the day. As I was driving, one of my friends would grab the cigarette lighter out of my dash and pretend it was a microphone while he sang along with the artists singing on WAKY radio. To us, that old AM radio sounded as good as the Syrus/XM satellite radios of today's automobiles.

After reading the book *Crash Club,* I decided that I wanted the phrase "to conquer or to die" on the engine of my '58 Chevy. (I know, I know – sounds like I wanted to be a caped crusader!) One night Bud and I raised the hood on that old black Chevy, and he lettered these words in Latin on the top of my radiator, "*Aut vincere, aut mori.*" Countless numbers of teenagers asked me, "What the crap does that mean?" It was my and Buddy's secret – only the two of us understood. When I traded in that Chevy, the written message was still on the radiator.

With all of the new technology of today's automobiles, when I raise the hood of my 2011 Ford Explorer Limited, I can hardly explain what function the maze of parts actually performs. It would be impossible now to even change the spark plugs of my automobiles. There is one feature, however, that I consider being a distinct advantage. Now that I have been exposed, I would find it difficult to do without: my 394-watt, high-definition, surround-sound, 12-speaker, Sony satellite radio/CD player.

All of my '50s and '60s rock and roll tunes have never sounded so good! Even Buddy Holly and Roy Orbison would be amazed at the clean sounds coming out of my 12 speakers. As the sounds come from the 50s channel or the 60s channel, I find myself turning up the volume and singing to the top of my lungs.

The days of "boys and their cars" will never again be like it was when I was a teenager. In those days, we could customize our rides for a few hundred dollars. A few months ago, I was attending an old car show and witnessed a gentleman offer the owner of a 1950 Mercury $30,000 for his car – the owner simply laughed. Oh, how I wish we could go back to those good old days of old time rock and roll and "hot rod" cars. Nevertheless, I am grateful to have the memories.

Kingsmen

Recently I was cleaning out a storage building that I had been using for the past 20 years when I came across a box of items from my high school days. Inside the box was an aluminum car-club plaque with the name *Kingsmen* engraved on the front. The memories came flowing back from the early 60s.

In 1960, I finally took my driver's test and became a teenager with a car on the road. I had been driving since I was approximately 12 so it had seemed like it was a lifetime until I could actually get my license. My first automobile ('58 Chevy) became my second home. When one of my friends told me that a new car club was forming, I was ecstatic.

I remember attending my first meeting in the parking lot of the Greyhound Bus Station across the street from the Mt. Vernon Cemetery. The following teenagers were also in attendance: Charles Hensley ('50 Chevy), Bud Cox ('31 Model A Ford), Billy Swinney ('50 Mercury), Clyde Wagner ('47 or '48 Chrysler), and "Snookie" Taylor ('30 Model A Ford). The crowd seemed larger in my memory, so I asked Bud Cox and Charles Hensley if they could remember any others at that meeting. Although they could not recall the names of any additional teens there, they agreed that there was a larger group than just the above.

Car clubs in America became popular at the end of World War II. Two well-liked magazines, *Rod and Custom* and *Hot Rod,* brought the idea of teenage car clubs into vogue. They provided many advertisements about custom car parts that could be ordered by the car-crazy youth of the day. The most popular catalog for teens was J.C. Whitney. Someone at the initial meeting had a Whitney catalog, and it was already turned to the page showing car club plaques, how they could be customized, and how much each of them cost.

I remember someone at the first meeting saying, "We need to decide tonight what our name is going to be so we can order our plaques to hang below our back bumpers." I remember Bud and Billy Swinney having the discussion about the plaques. Billy may have been leading the group that particular night. I cannot recall if he was the president of the club or not, but he played a leadership role. It took a great deal of time, but the group finally agreed to name our club *Kingsmen*. Unfortunately, I do not recall the reasoning for reaching that decision.

As I remember it, the next items on the agenda were to decide: the amount of membership dues, when the meetings were to be scheduled, and where we would meet on a regular basis. I vaguely recall that we had to put a dollar into a jar each time that we had a regular meeting. We also had to give Billy our money for the plaques so that he could place our first order. The monogrammed **Kingsmen** plates were priced at $2.50 each, which was a lot of money to me at the time.

I also remember being at another meeting when the plaques were distributed. We decided how many links of chain that each plate would hang upon between the bumper and the actual sign. Because I had lowered my Chevy so close to the ground, mine often dragged the pavement. When it did, it resulted in making sparks. Some clubs in *Hot Rod Magazine* called them "drag plates" – not because of drag racing, but because they would often drag when mounted on lowered automobiles like mine.

It was just too cool to be driving down Main Street in Mt. Vernon and see another member of the Kingsmen coming toward you. We always blew the horn and waved at other members. Because we were spending a lot of time together, we became close friends.

We also assisted each other when one of our cars needed some form of customizing. Bud and I worked on each other's cars on a regular basis. In those days, we always had a new idea about how to change our rides. Sometimes it would be something major like points and plugs, or another time we might simply be painting our wheels. Our cars were in need of perpetual attention.

When I was preparing to pen this story, I called Charles Hensley, who now lives in Arizona. He remembered having one of the plaques on his '50 Chevy. He also revealed that he is currently involved in a new auto club, which is called the **Fat Fender Fords**. This club is limited to '53 through '56 Ford pick-up trucks and panel trucks. Charles has a '56 panel truck that has been painted aqua and is most spectacular.

Charles suggested that I do a little research on aluminum car signs of the early '50s and '60s. Was I ever surprised! These keep-sakes have a collectability that is hard to believe. I saw photos of hundreds of such signs and discovered their value. The cheapest one that I could find was $90; some of them were priced at more than $300!

None of the guys with whom I conferred could remember the location of their own Kingsmen signs or even if they still existed. Could it be that mine is a "one of a kind" relic of the past organization? Regardless, I have fond memories of the long-gone society. For some reason, the club provided us a way to demonstrate how proud we were of our cars – and I guess to show-off a little as the guys who drove them. And, of course, it didn't hurt that even the girls thought the group was very cool.

Weren't those the days?!

Date Night – Summer 1960

The following is how I remember being on a special date during the summer of 1960. I was a sophomore at Mt. Vernon High School.

At that time, I was working on Saturdays, delivering groceries for my Uncle Jesse Cummins' grocery store on Main Street in Mt. Vernon. When I got off work, I quickly took my '58 Chevy to the Chevron station behind the courthouse in order to give my car a thorough wash job. I always thought that a clean automobile was a necessity when taking out one of my girlfriends. When my Chevy met my specifications, I hurried home to take a bath for the upcoming date. I dressed in my best Levi jeans, a clean button-down shirt, and my Bass Weejuns.

By the time I had cleaned my car and myself, it was time to cruise down Main Street to see who else was planning a date for the night. As I expected, several of my friends were also out cruising before picking up their dates. Oscar Fain, Jim Barton Nunnelley, and Bud Cox were sitting at the Dinner Bell Restaurant waiting for the 7 o'clock hour to pick up their dates. We exchanged plans for the evening. Then I noticed that it was already 6:45, so I cranked up my Chevy and headed for the home of Barbara Sue Mullins's grandmother. As was customary, I walked up the sidewalk and knocked on the door. Barbara Sue met me at the door and invited me to come inside. After exchanging small talk, we left and headed for my car.

Since it was still bright daylight, we decided to drive around to see which of our friends were out on the streets on this Saturday evening before heading for the Valley Drive-in Theater. As we drove down Richmond Avenue, we met several of my friends: Paul Daily, Charles Hensley, Charles Bennett Farris, and Jim Cox; each of them blew his horn as we passed.

Barbara Sue suggested we drive out to Hamm's Drive-in Restaurant to see who else might be around consuming their famous burgers and fries. We pulled into a spot and ordered dinner from the car. In the background, we could hear the jukebox playing "Chances Are" by Johnny Mathis. When the jukebox stopped, we turned up my AM radio and listened to WAKY out of Louisville. Everyone knew that some of the best rock and roll could be heard on Saturday night on that station.

Just at that moment, Sam Cooke's "You Send Me" began to play, and Barbara Sue again turned up the volume on my radio – and a smile spread across my face.

After downing our burgers and fries, we decided to drive around a little longer before heading to the movie. Back in Mt. Vernon, we stopped to chat with Oscar Fain and Helen, who were also planning a night at the drive-in theater.

As the sun began to set on the horizon, Barbara Sue suggested, "We'd better go so we can get a good spot at the movie." I agreed, of course, and off we went toward Renfro Valley. On our way down US 25, we cranked up the volume on the radio and sang with all our hearts along with Roy Orbison, Elvis, The Platters, and Jerry Lee Lewis. We both knew the words to every song, and louder and louder we sang the words to the music pounding out of my two speakers. About this time, Barbara Sue slid across my front bench seat to take her place by my side. Once again, a grin appeared on my face.

As we pulled into the theater entrance, Barbara Sue, who had not questioned which movie we were seeing, noticed that the movie listed on the marquee was Alfred Hitchcock's *Psycho*. "David Joe, this is supposed to be a very scary movie," she says. My reply: "Yes," I said, quickly adding, "but I have heard that it is supposed to be a really good flick. I think it has been nominated for an Oscar."

We carefully selected just the right parking spot, several rows behind the concession stand. Before the movie was to begin, I made my way to the concession stand to get us some popcorn and Cokes. When I came back to the car, I couldn't help but notice that Barbara Sue was still sitting in the middle of the front seat – and I smiled once again. Throughout the previews of coming attractions and the cartoons, we made small talk and caught up on what was happening in each other's lives since we were last together. (At that time, she was living in Ohio, and we had limited time to be able to be with each other on weekends.)

Once the movie had started, we slid the seat back and got comfortable. Everything was going great until Janet Leigh registered at the Bates Motel. From that point on Barbara Sue, with fear on her face, gripped my hand like a vice. When Anthony Perkins ripped open the shower curtain, female screams from all around the drive-in joined with hers. But, being such a manly date, I held Barbara Sue with all my might, reassuring her, "Everything is alright!" This was a great movie to bring a girl to!

When the movie was over, Barbara Sue was positioned as closely to my side as possible. I slowly drove out of the theater entrance and turned right, heading toward Renfro Valley. Just past the Renfro Valley Lodge, we turned left onto a small gravel road and made our way up the hill into the parking lot of the Red Bud School House. This was a popular spot to watch the "submarine races."

I tuned the radio to WLS in Chicago for some good rock and roll tunes being played by Dick Biondi. One of the first songs that I remember playing was "Never Be Anyone Else But You" by Ricky Nelson. The evening continued, with an excellent performance by the submarines. When Roy Orbison began to sing "Only the Lonely," Barbara Sue suggested that we had better be getting on home. Reluctantly, I started up my Chevy and headed back to Mt. Vernon.

Barbara Sue held my hand all the way to her house, and when we finally pulled into her driveway, she said, "I hate for the evening to be over." That was absolutely my sentiment, too. I walked her to the door and gave her a last kiss goodnight. As I left, she stood in the door and watched as I drove away.

As most of the guys did after such an evening, I decided to check out who all was at the Chevron. Pulling into the station parking lot,

I saw that inside were Charles Hensley, Lloyd Fain, and Bobby Joe Sweeney. We all hung out for probably an hour, reviewing the courses that each of our dates had taken. While heading home on US 25, I thought about what a good time that I had that night.

I thought about the night and about Barbara Sue. She would be leaving for Ohio early the next morning, and I was missing her already. It wouldn't be long before I would receive a letter from her recounting how much fun we had together and advising me as to when she would be returning in Rockcastle County. I was always more than ready for her return. To me, she was a very special date.

Me with some friends

Hamm's Drive-In Restaurant

Warm summer evenings, cruising Hamm's Drive-in – the memory of this gathering place for Rockcastle County teenagers lingers in my mind. It was a great place for guys to meet chicks, exchange phone numbers, or to set up dates for the following weekend. Having a smiling carhop bring burgers, fries, and a Coke to your car was also pretty cool. Hamm's was one of the best places around to hang out and listen to good old rock and roll music.

A few days ago, my good friend Bud Cox and I were discussing the days when we frequented Hamm's while we were teenagers attending Mt. Vernon High School in the early '60s. One of the memories that stands out for both of us was the fine-looking automobiles that could be seen on any given weekend in the parking lot.

Buddy recalled, "Because the parking lot was gravel, you had to look out for mud holes if you had just washed your car." I distinctly remember the parking lot and agreed that finding just the right parking spot was critical. In those days, I washed my black '58 Chevy at least twice a week in order to attract the female persuasion when cruising Hamm's and other teenage attractions in the county.

Bud usually drove his 1960 Plymouth Valiant or a 1955 Ford at that time. I remember helping Bud put black electrical tape on the grill of that Valiant to give it a customized look. The two of us were together a lot during those magical days.

Bud also reminisced about the jukebox inside Hamm's Drive In. "You had to go inside to play the jukebox, but the speakers were outside so you could sit in your car and listen to the music," he said. I cannot begin to count the times that Bud and I drove out US 150 toward Brodhead to visit Hamm's in order to check out who was there and to sample that fine cuisine known as burgers and fries.

Hamm's was owned by Harris and Ruby Hiatt Hamm, who were also the uncle and aunt of my friend Jerry Hamm. Jerry was a few years older than I was, but we both loved old cars and driving all over Rockcastle County. Jerry was lucky enough to marry one of the cutest cheerleaders that ever attended Mt. Vernon High School – Carol Jean Owens. She and I were also friends and hung out together when she did not have a date with Jerry.

In those days, most teenagers took their dates to Hamm's on the weekends. One of my memories includes how neat it was to have bench seats in our cars, allowing us to cuddle in the front seat. When the car hop came to take your order, she only had to visit the driver's window, because the girls were usually sitting next to the boys who were driving. Of course, none of us had air conditioning in our cars, and the windows were always rolled down. Having the windows down also made it possible to hear the sounds coming from the jukebox inside.

Inside Hamm's were tables – in case you did not want to dine in your car. There was also a counter with bar stools which lined one wall. In addition to the jukebox, there were pinball machines to play (if you did not have a date).

Next door to Hamm's was a building that housed a pool room where guys without dates congregated on Saturday nights. As you can imagine, that part of US 150 was very popular with the teens of Rockcastle County, plus it was only approximately three miles from Brodhead and Mt. Vernon. Teens from both high schools gathered at the drive-in restaurant to chat, check out the cars, look for girls, and feast on the latest fast food.

After the carhops came to the window to take our orders, they returned in about fifteen minutes with our hot burgers and fries. The food was delivered on a special tray that fit on the door of our cars; the food was wrapped in paper and was extremely hot and tasty. There was just something special about the taste of food delivered by a carhop – another marker in my mind of the early '60s. *"Those were the days*," as Nat King Cole sang through our drive-in speakers.

My wife, Kathy, and I love to visit the Smoky Mountains several times each year, and we have found our own modern version of an old-fashioned drive-in restaurant in Pigeon Forge, Tennessee. It is called Mel's Diner, and we go there as often as we can. Although it does not actually have car service, the food is very 1960s and so is the atmosphere. Hanging on the walls are "golden records" of many of the singers we listened to while at Hamm's. One of the best parts of Mel's is the jukebox that belts out a variety of "oldies but goodies" – with a sign hanging nearby proclaiming that if the music is too loud, you are in the wrong place.

Many of the menu items at Mel's are named for celebrities from the '50s and '60s, such as the Marilyn Monroe burger or some Chubby Checker fries. Even the waitresses remind me of my Hamm's Drive-in days. They wear tee-shirts like we did, and they are always extremely friendly. Mel's also blasts rock and roll out into the parking lot. That place takes me back to the days when Bud and I were hanging out at Hamm's.

Any baby boomer has memories of a place like this – there was one in virtually every town back then. Although there are some drive-in restaurants around today, they are not the same. Hamm's, like so many others, was dominated by energetic and hungry teens – those places were *ours*.

Midnight Rendezvous

I receive a lot of my topic inspirations from the music that I listen to as I relax, drive, or work at my computer. I take my iPod with me no matter where I go, and it contains 4,800 of my favorite songs. A good number of the tunes are either vintage rock-and-roll or country.

While recently listening to Alan Jackson's *Chattahoochee,* I was reminded of the "midnight rendezvous" with my high school friends on Friday and Saturday nights after we took our dates home. In those days, girls had early curfew hours, and the guys found that they had some time on their hands before going home for the night.

Jackson bluntly describes the events of those kinds of evenings. As I listened, I couldn't help but think he was talking about the '60s and the places where my friends and I met. He sings about the early part of the evening:

> *Well we fogged up the windows in my old Chevy*
> *I was willin' but she wasn't ready*
> *So I settled for a burger and a grape snow cone*
> *Dropped her off early but I didn't go home.*

Most of the guys actually drove Chevys, and we predetermined where to meet after the ladies were delivered safely home. There were three spots that we frequented: Baker's Standard Oil, the Dinner Bell Restaurant parking lot, and the Water Works Lake (The Dam).

Jackson even knows what we talked about on those nights when we gathered around our cars.

> *...in the pale moonlight*
> *Talkin' bout cars and dreamin' bout women*
> *Never had a plan, just livin' for the minute.*

Sometimes we got bored and piled into one of the cars to drive the 18 miles to Berea College, seeking entertainment until we had to go home. One night Paul, Bobby Joe, Charles, and Lloyd joined me in my '58 Chevy, and we took a tour of the campus in Berea. We were looking for the more mature college co-eds who may have decided to take a walk before going to bed. We finally settled on burgers and fries at Elkin's Drive-In Restaurant without much success in the co-ed department.

While at the restaurant, we were noticed by a couple of guys in a customized '55 Chevy who wanted to test our skills in the "drag racing" department. Of course, we couldn't let the dare go. We told them to follow us to the "Fairview Stretch" of US 25.

I got out of my car and removed the exhaust caps to set those horses free. One of my friends became the starter, and one of the other guys got out at the end of the quarter-mile marker. Again, Jackson recounts the proceedings of the night.

> *We layed rubber*
> *On the (Kentucky) asphalt*
> *We got a little crazy but we never got caught.*

I clearly remember seeing the tail lights of the '55 as we crossed the finish line. I never had a chance. (He was driving a V-8, and I had a 6-cylinder.) My friend Charles commented, "Next time, we will bring my '51 Chevy and see how they feel." He had a 6-cylinder too, but Charles was a mechanical wizard. His '51 had been altered and would have competed well.

When I finally pulled into the driveway at home, my mother was standing at the kitchen door waiting for me as she always did. In all the years before I left for college, she never failed to greet me when

I came home. Unlike in some homes, there was no hassle. She just wanted to make sure that I was alright before she could relax and go to bed. Sometimes she would say, "It's pretty late, isn't it son?!" (That blessed woman probably prayed me out of lots of dangerous situations.)

And, yes, it was usually a bit late before the guys all headed home. But the night had been complete – chicks in the early part of the evening; then a rendezvous with the guys, our cars, and sometimes a drag race or two. It was a charmed life – and we didn't even know it.

Midnight Run to Bristol

I recently received an e-mail from Sam Barnes, who is a friend of mine from my high school days. He reminded me of an event from our youth that I had not thought about in a very long time: a late-night trip to Bristol, Tennessee, taken by several of us when we were full-force teenage boys.

In those days (1961), the guys would occasionally tell their parents that we were staying over at the home of one of our friends – and then simply drive around all night as a sort of adventure. This particular escapade involved Sam, Gary Coffey, Paul Daily, Marion Whitehouse, and me. Early that evening we decided to take a trip in my '58 Chevrolet with (as Chuck Berry says) *"no particular place to go."*

Each of us called home to explain that we were staying overnight with one another; we then pooled our funds and took off on our journey. For the life of me, I cannot explain why we chose Bristol, but off we went.

I remember driving down US 25 until we got to London, and from there we stayed on KY 80 until we were almost to Hazard. At that point, we took US 421 right into the middle of Bristol.

The radio was tuned to WLS in Chicago, and we sang along with DJ Dick Biondi as he played the Top 40 songs of the day. Since my Chevrolet did not have air conditioning, all of the windows were rolled down. As a result, we serenaded everyone from Mt. Vernon to the border town of Bristol, Tennessee, and Bristol, Virginia.

A sign welcomed us to the twin cities. The state line ran down the middle of the street – Tennessee on one side and Virginia on the other. Too cool.

When we reached our destination, the guys were starving. I pulled off to the side of the road, and we surveyed our financial situation. Keeping enough funds for the gasoline for our return trip to Rockcastle County, we pooled the rest of our money – only to discover that we did not have enough for all of us to order a meal.

Someone who was looking out of the side window announced, "There's a doughnut shop just up the road." It was a solution that allowed everyone to eat. We purchased a large sack of glazed doughnuts and some Cokes for us to share.

I have no idea what the population of Bristol was at the time, but it was considerably larger than Mt. Vernon (which then was 1,106). We continued to drive around the city trying to find something to get into like most boys of our age always did. A group of local teenagers started to follow us, and one of our group suggested that we out-run them.

I was afraid to get a ticket in Tennessee/Virginia, so I took a quick left turn and, to my surprise, started down a railroad track. I must say that I'll never forget that. We bumped along the track until we came to the next street, where I took a quick right turn and noticed that the boys had not followed us. We never did find any girls.

Gary Coffey reminded us that we had to get back home in time for school the next morning. So we bid a farewell to Bristol, and up US 421 we drove toward Big Stone Gap. Just inside the border of Kentucky, one of the boys recommended that we stop at a small truck stop in order to use the restroom.

By this time, I was hungry again. When I saw that the establishment sold canned vegetables, I bought four cans of beanie weenies. In order to make the beans and weenies edible, we placed them on the manifold of the engine to warm them up. One of the guys picked up some crackers from the restaurant, so we had beans, crackers, and two Cokes to share.

The guys slept all the way home while I drove listening to the radio. When we got to Rockcastle County, I stopped at the truck stop just up from Pine Hill so that we could clean up a bit in order to look presentable for school. One of the guys found enough change to buy some Dentyne gum – a means of refreshing our "beanie weenie" breath before going to homeroom.

Throughout the day, it was all we could do to stay awake. All of us looked like we had been "ridden hard and put away wet." I kept thinking about my bed and how good it would feel to slide between the sheets. It felt like the day would never end!

When I got home, Bee had prepared a scrumptious dinner, but I was so tired I could hardly eat. She kept prodding me about my night at Gary Coffey's and why I was so exhausted. I told her that we were up late playing games, and I just wanted to go to bed. She believed me.

The next day was Saturday so I slept all day long. That night the guys and I relived our jaunt – and then started planning our next excursion. You know, boys will be boys.

My '63 Chevy

My '63 Super Sport
Was Sweet

While traveling to Lexington on the interstate, a classic 1963 Chevrolet passed me, and my mind immediately brought memories of the first new automobile that I ever owned. That beauty will always be my favorite "ride" of all time.

Throughout high school, I worked at several jobs around my hometown. In the summers and on weekends, I pumped gas for my dad at his filling station and for Bakers' Chevron. On Saturdays I delivered groceries for my uncle Jesse Cummins. Most of the money that I made went directly to finance my automobiles.

A black '58 Chevy was the first used car that I owned, and I truly loved that car. But by 1963, I was preparing to leave Mt. Vernon to attend UK, and I was more than ready to move up to a brand new set of wheels.

My grandfather, who had previously assisted my older brother with a car purchase, volunteered to help me with mine as well. The following Saturday, we were off to Briton's Chevrolet to do some pricing. Like many folks looking to buy a new vehicle, we did not leave before making a deal.

With Pop's help, my savings, and my trade-in, I was on my way to owning (outright – no financing!) a sweet, baby blue, 1963 Impala Super Sport. Pop let me go through the process of ordering the car that I wanted while he just sat and listened as Mr. Briton and I went through the details.

After we finished, Pop said, "Mr. Briton, give me the best offer you can for my grandson's first car." He spent a long time entering figures into his adding machine and finally handed Pop a piece of paper with an amount written on it. I strained to see the figure but Pop kept it folded. Then he said, "On the square, is that the best price you can give us?" (I later learned that this expression was one that fellow Masons used with one another.) Mr. Briton replied that it was, and Pop told him to order the car.

When we got into my '58 Chevy for our ride home, I asked Pop how much the new car was going to cost. He then let me see the order that he had received from Mr. Briton. The price was $3,200.

Pop then began to question me about some of the accessories I had ordered. He had not understood much of the terminology. He said, "What are bucket seats?" I explained. Then he fired another question, "What is a four in the floor?" The look on his face was priceless when I explained that the shifting lever would be mounted on the floor between the bucket seats. He replied, "That is how they used to be years ago!"

The next question was, "Why do you want a V-8?" It was hard to make him understand the value of a 327 cubic inch engine, especially when he always bought six-cylinder automobiles. I did not volunteer the information that I also ordered a positive-traction rear end and the Super Sport package.

He did notice that the engine had a four-barrel carburetor and simply noted, "You will not get good mileage with that hot engine!" That, of course, was of no consequence whatsoever to me. (Ah, the good ole days of cheap gas!)

For the next six weeks, I waited for Pop to call to let me know that my car had finally arrived. It was probably the longest six weeks of my life. At long last, he called and said, "Dave, you'd better come home this weekend so we can pick up your new car." By the following Saturday, I was in my new ride. The drive home was very exciting to me, but Pop just hung on and did not comment on my new "hot" automobile.

After a few weeks, I began to customize my new car. First, I added fender skirts, dual chrome exhaust extensions, and exhaust cut-out caps. My new baby was so sweet, and I loved touring around Rockcastle County looking for my friends to take them for a ride.

Back at UK, I could hardly wait to get a date with a girl I had been flirting with so I could show her my new Super Sport. The look on her face when I picked her up for the first time was enough to make my day! That may have been the first time that I was sorry to have ordered bucket seats. That night at the drive-in theatre in Lexington, lots of teenagers came up to look at my new car. I am quite sure that I was beaming with pride.

Today, that exact model and year can be had for a mere $42,000. If I had only loved that baby enough to keep hold of her....

Rock 'n Roll

Courtesy of American Bandstand Archives

American Bandstand

When I was only 13, American Bandstand first aired on ABC Television on Monday, August 5, 1957. The show ran Monday through Friday from 3:00 to 4:30pm – just in time for teenagers to get home from school, plant themselves in front of the TV, and tune in to see the latest rock and roll artists perform their hits. The show was hosted by the clean-cut, 26-year-old Dick Clark, and it became a smashing success.

The small, black and white, wooden-encased television set in our living room became my center of attention each afternoon. Bee made sure that snacks were available for me and my friends who gathered to watch. Not all of my friends had television sets, and many of them came home with me in order to view the show that had quickly become all the rage.

As the show's popularity grew, so did the number of teens who gathered around their sets after school in Mt. Vernon. Usually, we scooted the coffee table back and actually tried to mimic the dancing on the screen.

I specifically remember being at Sandy Murrell's house with several of our friends and dancing with the TV set providing the music. Sandy's father, Fred, came into the living room and asked us to "hold the noise down." That lasted for all of about 10 minutes, and we then turned the volume back up. (I think he went out and sat on the porch until we had to go home for dinner.)

Dick Clark had an amazing rapport with the teens on the show. Each day, part of the show dealt with clothing trends, favorite songs, and dance fads. He also chose a couple of the teens to rate a record.

Because of his young age, he was not seen as an "outsider" and, in many ways, he became just part of the crowd.

The teenagers on the show were mostly "regulars" who had been chosen to appear on the program. The girls were not allowed to wear slacks or tight sweaters, and the boys were mandated to wear a coat and tie. Smoking and chewing gum were totally banned. As a result, parents and adults basically had no complaints about the program since it was a squeaky clean portrayal of the young.

The success of the show was in part due to the artists who performed among the kids. American Bandstand soon became the showcase for such major talents as Frankie Avalon, Bobby Darin, Connie Francis, Fabian, Chuck Berry, Jerry Lee Lewis, Buddy Holly, and Chubby Checker.

Hank Ballard, a rhythm and blues singer/songwriter who was an early rocker with his backup group, the Midnighters, summed up Clark's success: "The man was big. He was the biggest thing in America at the time. He was bigger than the President." With the large number of TV viewers, having a song played on the Bandstand virtually guaranteed that thousands of copies of the record would be sold within the next week. A record played daily had a good chance of going "Top Ten."

A little-known fact: Two of the biggest stars of the time never appeared on the Bandstand. Elvis Presley did not need the show for his success. And Ricky Nelson was already a hit from his performances on his family's show, *The Adventures of Ozzie and Harriet.*

The teens from Mt. Vernon learned many new dance steps by watching the show. In 1959 Clark featured the Twist on his show, performed by Chubby Checker. The song had originally been the B-side of Hank Ballard's single, "Teardrops on Your Letter." It became an immediate hit with the teens on Bandstand. Checker's rendition became the number one song on the singles chart in the United States in 1960 and then again in 1962.

From that day on, every time we gathered to dance at one of our homes, we "twisted the night away." As I recall, some of my friends became quite good at it, including Bud Cox, Bobby Joe Sweeney, Carla Baker, and Sandy Murrell.

In 1961, a local New York band, Joey Dee and the Starliters, were performing at the Peppermint Lounge, and their hit "The Peppermint Twist" became number one on the Top 40 charts for three weeks. While on my senior trip to New York, a couple of us visited the Peppermint Lounge and got to see Joey Dee. It was a real thrill to witness. (The senior trip advisors never even missed us.)

By 1964, ABC moved Bandstand from weekdays to Saturdays, turning it into a weekly, hour-long show. Clark then moved the location of the show's filming from Philadelphia to Hollywood. During that time, The Beatles and what became known as the "British Invasion" began dominating the music scene.

Clark maintained the basic format of the show that he had developed in the 1950s. Today, that show retains its position as the longest-running broadcast aimed at youth to air on American television. After 30 years of broadcasting, ABC finally dropped the show from its network schedule in 1987. In 1993, Dick Clark was inducted into the Rock and Roll Hall of Fame.

I believe that American Bandstand played a substantial role in my passion for rock and roll music – as it did for many teens of the era. It provided those of us who were fans a stage to witness some of the greatest early stars of the music that we claimed as ours. Dick and the Bandstand gave us the feeling of being a part of something special that was evolving right before our very eyes and ears. In my mind, we were all a part of American Bandstand.

Bobby Joe Sweeney

Gene Vincent & His Blue Caps (Croydon Municipal)

Stereo Arrived with "Be-Bop-A-Lula"

While traveling recently on US 25 between Mt. Vernon and Berea and listening to an "old time rock-and-roll" station, I heard "Be-Bop-A-Lula" by Gene Vincent & His Blue Caps. Those of you who are not hip to 50s and 60s music must be thinking, "Gene who?" Well, since you asked, allow me to explain my sudden rush of excitement upon hearing that song. Gene recorded it in 1955, and it climbed up the "Top-40" charts. By 1956, it was playing on radio stations all across the US.

At that time, I was 12 years old and had just purchased my first *stereo* record player at Bryant's Hardware store on Main Street in Mt. Vernon. Stereo was all the rage with teenagers because you could hear the music coming out of one speaker and the singer out of the other. Even though we were captured by the separation of sound, some RCA executives declared that "the stereo sound" was merely a passing fancy and that mono would be the standard in the record business.

I will always remember that Gene Vincent's hit was on my first stereo album. I sat in front of those separated speakers and listened to it play over and over and over again. I was totally flipped. (That's "excited" to those of you who are not hip to the jive!)

My mother finally exclaimed, "David Joe, you are gonna wear that record out!" She was accustomed to the old 78-rpm records that her generation had listened to several years before my "new fangled" record player arrived on the scene. Her favorites were Perry Como, Frank Sinatra, and Bing Crosby. I remember stacking my 45s on my new player, too, as I listened to "Blueberry Hill" by Fats Domino, "The Great Pretender" by The Platters, "Love Me Tender" by the one and only Elvis, and "Blue Suede Shoes" by Carl Perkins – which were all hits of 1956.

Over the next few years, my record collection grew as more and more rock and roll stars released hit songs. By the time I was 16 and could drive, it was the fad to gather at one of our homes in order to listen to the latest "chart toppers" and dance the night the away. One night we were invited to Nancy Helton's house, and there were probably 40-50 teenagers dancing to our tunes by the time her mom pushed us out the door.

When I became a junior in high school, my grandfather gave me permission to convert one of our smokehouses into a "club" for my friends. The building was approximately 25 x 30 feet. It had electricity, and a single bare bulb hung from the center of the ceiling. It was to become our new hang-out.

Bud Cox and I gathered cardboard boxes for days and completely covered the inside walls so that we could paint. We selected "Lavender Blue" (do you remember?) as the color. My mother made some red curtains for the only window. We put red light bulbs in the lamps and hung one from the middle of the room. A small coal stove sat in the corner. We gathered as much "furniture" as we could squeeze inside – like an old army cot with a folded blanket on top for seating. In another corner, we strategically placed the stereo.

Within a few days, our friends burned rubber getting to the "pad." The place was just toooo cooool! On special occasions, my mother would prepare sandwiches, chips and pickles, and Cokes for my guests. (And I will admit that there might have been an occasion or two when a couple of dating couples used the club for necking rather than dancing.)

Those truly were fun times. Such simple times. We did not require lots of expensive forms of entertainment. We were satisfied just spending time with our friends, listening to our music, and dancing. Even Gene Vincent kept it simple:

> *Well, be-bop-a-lula she's my baby*
> *Be-bop-a-lula I don't mean maybe*

Well, she's the girl in the red blue jeans
She's the queen of all the teens
She's the one woman that I know
She's the one that loves me so...

Be-bop-a-lula she's my baby now.

Me, as a high school graduate

Rock and Roll – the Soundtrack of My Life

"Rock Around the Clock" was barely heard above the crowd of wild teenagers in the 1955 movie *Blackboard Jungle*, which we watched at the Vernon Theatre. For many, the song became the anthem of the '50s youth, and it is widely considered to be the song that, more than any other, brought rock and roll into mainstream culture in America.

I had not even reached my teenage years when I witnessed this phenomenon. I had no idea how this new music would affect my life over the next fifty-plus years. "Rock Around the Clock" generated much controversy in the press of the time and an uproar among the youth of the day. That song, along with Allen Freed's Cleveland-based radio show, gave the name to this form of music – Rock And Roll.

There are countless times when the music of my youth plays in my mind of remembrance. One such example was a fall Saturday afternoon when Pop and I were strolling in the woods behind his house. I, of course, was listening to my AM transistor radio when Bobby Darin began to sing "Mack the Knife."

> *Oh, the shark, babe, has such teeth, dear*
> *And it shows them pearly white*
> *Just a jackknife has old MacHeath, babe*
> *And he keeps it, ah, out of sight…*

. . . .

And someone's sneaking 'round the corner
Could that someone be Mack the Knife?

Pop asked, "What in the world is he singing about? That sounds like garbage to me!" He had no idea that the song in question was moving quickly toward the top of the Rock and Roll Top 40 charts. He and most of his age group could not understand our fascination with this new music. To us, it was a style of music that was just plain old fun. The year was 1959.

Another song that always brings back specific memories of the 50s to me is Gene Vincent's "Be-Bop-A-Lula."

Well, be-bop-a-lula, she's my baby
Be-bop-a-lula, I don't mean maybe…
Well, she's the girl in the red blue jeans
She's the queen of all the teens
She's the one that I know
She's the one that loves me so

That song was on the first album that I ever purchased. My friend Bud Cox and I wore that record out letting it play over and over on my first stereo record player and – with a speaker that extended to the other side of the room! In those days the separation of music and voices was such a novelty. We would say to each other, "Listen to the guitar in this speaker!" That year was 1956.

I suppose the most memorial Rock and Roll event to me as a young man was the death of Buddy Holly on February 3, 1959. He has been described as "the single most influential creative force in early Rock and Roll." In February of 1957, his single "That'll Be the Day" became the number-one hit of the year. I knew every word of the lyrics. I walked around the house singing,

Well, that'll be the day, when you say goodbye
Yes, that'll be the day, when you make me cry
You say you're gonna leave, you know it's a lie
'Cause that'll be the day when I die.

Mommie Katie was a staunch Christian and taught Bible classes at Mt. Vernon Baptist Church. One day she heard me singing that song and said, "David Joe, you should not sing about dying. You know that is not right!" Of course, I never again sang that song in her presence.

In 1958 Elvis Presley released a tune about a newly developed fad that was sweeping the nation – the practice of "going steady." Each one knew where the other one was at all times. There were also tokens of the relationship – a school letter sweater or a ring. His song, "Won't You Wear My Ring Around Your Neck" made it to the number two song on the pop charts.

> *Won't you wear my ring around your neck*
> *To tell the world I'm yours, by heck*
> *Let them see your love for me*
> *And let them see by the ring around your neck.*

Many of my friends and I allowed our rings to be worn by our newest girlfriends. For some reason, that particular token gave us some comfort knowing we had a date for each up-coming event. In other words, *tell the world I'm yours, by heck!*

Now that I have reached the autumn of my life, I still find that Rock and Roll songs express my emotions better than I can verbally. For instance, my wife and I just recently celebrated our 32nd wedding anniversary, and a song best describes how I feel about her. It is Eric Clapton's "Wonderful Tonight":

> *It's late in the evening; she's wondering what clothes to*
> *   wear.*
> *She puts on her make-up and brushes her long blond hair.*
> *And then she asks me, "Do I look all right?"*
> *And I say, "Yes, you look wonderful tonight."*
>
> *We go to a party and everyone turns to see*
> *This beautiful lady that's walking around with me.*
> *And then she asks me, "Do you feel alright?"*
> *And I say, "Yes, I feel wonderful tonight."*

I feel wonderful because I see
The love light in your eyes.
And the wonder of it all
Is that you just don't realize
how much I love you.

(Call it "mush" if you will, gentlemen, the ladies will understand.) I am long past caring what others think, and frankly it is my opinion that we should let our loved ones know how we feel.) This is my way.

Bill Haley and The Comets

"I like That Old-Time Rock and Roll"

I was a boy when rock and roll was born in the United States. Music experts say that "Rock Around the Clock," by Bill Haley and The Comets was the first rock and roll song. The movie of the same name played at the Vernon Theatre in Mt. Vernon, Kentucky, my home town, and I was there.

I had always lived in a community that was associated with Renfro Valley and country music, so the birth of rock was very exciting to me. Because we were so close to Memphis, many of the Sun Recording artists played on the local radio station, WRVK. My favorite stars at the time included Jerry Lee Lewis, Carl Perkins, Fats Domino, and of course Elvis.

When WRVK radio went off the air at sundown, we would listen to WLS in Chicago. When I was in high school, the cool program on WLS was listening to disk jockey Dick Biondi from 9:00pm until midnight. There we were introduced to the likes of Buddy Holly, Roy Orbison, The Drifters, The Everly Brothers, and Jackie Wilson. We would drive our cars to the top of Green Fish Hill in order to get the best reception on our AM radios. Sometimes we would have six or eight cars gathered, and then other times there would be only one.

Another highlight of my high school days that involves rock was going to the skating rink in Berea. It was the super cool thing to do. We had our own shoe skates, and we danced (or skated) to the best rock and roll of the day. The rink had a great sound system and dance lights. We went every Thursday and Friday nights. From 8:00pm until midnight, we skated the night away. The rink always played two fast songs and then one slow number for cuddling. You can imagine the fun of jitterbugging to "Great Balls O'Fire." As the night grew later, more requests were for slow songs, such as "Chances Are" by Johnny Mathis or "Loving You" by the King.

I have always remained a rock and roll fan. As a young man, I loved going to concerts. One of my favorites was Bob Seger and the Silver Bullet Band. I saw him at Rupp Arena in 1978. I think his song "Old Time Rock and Roll" sums up my feelings about rock and roll music precisely. "*Just take those old records off the shelf....I'll sit and listen to them by myself, and be reminded of my days of old. Many might say I'm old fashioned and over the hill, which I may be, but that music fills my soul. I still love that old time rock and roll!*"

Several years ago, I was having a discussion with some of my friends and one of them asked, "If you were on a deserted island and could only listen to one artist, who would it be?" Without hesitation, I immediately said Bob Seger. The lyrics of many of his songs take you back to a younger time in your life. If your past memories are pleasant, then those lyrics give you glimpses of how much fun it used to be. For instance, His song "Like A Rock" describes an 18-year-old teenager who, "*never felt so strong...I stood proud and I stood tall.*" Then, when the teenager became 38, he says, "*20 years – where did they go?*" I can relate to that. I often ask myself, where did all those years go?

But when you want to re-visit those past times, you can "*just take those old records off the shelf*" (or these days the CDs that have replaced them) and listen to them and be transported back to your youth! That fact comforts me somehow.

Bob Seger (Courtesy of www.last.fm)

Buddy Holly (buddyhollystuff.tumblr.com)

The Day the Music Died

One day while driving home from work, I heard on the radio a tribute to Buddy Holly, Ritchie Valens, and The Big Bopper (J.R. Richardson). It was on February 3, 1959, that the fatal plane crash occurred just outside Clear Lake, Iowa.

I remember the following morning well. At that time, one of my friends from high school, Jim Barton Nunnelley, had a paper route. He occasionally asked me ride with him on his Moped scooter to help deliver the *Courier Journal* in Mt. Vernon. That morning the shock of the headline was overwhelming. When we picked up the papers, we learned that the three had been killed the night before.

Buddy was such a huge part of our lives at that time. We searched the radio for each of his recordings. Buddy Holly and the Crickets' first record, "That'll Be the Day" (1957) had sold over a million copies. Two other recordings, "Peggy Sue" and "Early in the Morning," were also chart toppers. At the time of his death, Holly (22) had produced three albums.

Over the years, that fatal day has been referred to as The Day the Music Died. Don McLean's 1971 song, "American Pie," contains many references to this day, including the phrase itself. The entire song is a tribute to Buddy Holly and a commentary on how rock and roll changed in the years following his death. "American Pie" reached number one on the music charts in the US in 1972.

Because of my association as a teenager with the newspaper delivery, this song brings back an eerie feeling each time I hear it played. These words from McLean's song will explain the reference:

...But February made me shiver,
with every paper I'd deliver,
Bad news on the doorstep...
I couldn't take one more step.
...But something touched me deep inside,
The day the music died.

Our loss was very real. In those days, listening to rock and roll and dancing were two of the mainstays of being a teenager. We did not have the luxury of iPods, cell phones, DVD players, and many other electronic gadgets that young people have today. In 1957 our choices were listening to AM "Top 40" or playing our records – and listen we did! It was common to gather at one of our homes and "jitterbug" the night away. Parents welcomed us and would prepare snacks for us to devour as we listened to one stack of 45s after another. By the way, those records cost 99 cents a piece. Two songs for a dollar! We would:

... kick off our shoes and
... dig those rhythm 'n' blues.

Buddy was sort of a hero for us at that time. He was young, brash, talented, and from a small town (Lubbock) in Texas. We identified with him. He started as a country singer and soared into popularity as a rock and roll star. Many of the girls at Mt. Vernon High School cried all day when we returned to school after his death. It was the talk of the week among our friends and even teachers.

I suppose we were witnessing a genius in the music business and we didn't even realize it. Holly's popularity has continued over the years. Many artists have recorded covers of his recordings. A hugely popular movie was made about his life. Oldie radio stations play his music on a regular basis.

Recently, I read an account of the last performance that Buddy made in Clear Lake, Iowa. He was describing the night and said, "We had as much fun as the kids did!" If that statement was true, then he must have had a great time performing his last concert. One thing is certain: we who were teens at that time will never forget The Day the Music Died.

The Big Bopper, Richie Valens, Buddy Holly

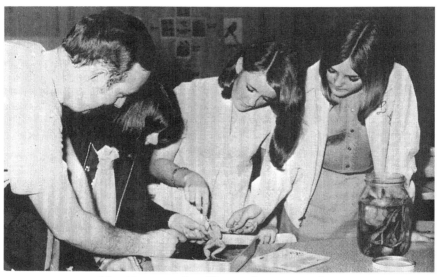

Me with some of my Human Anatomy students

Sweet Success

1969 Trojan Football Team
Class A State Champions

August Football Memories

When the first week of August rolls around, I can't help but recall my days of coaching high school football and the excitement of starting a new season. The air was filled with the popping of pads, the enthusiasm of experienced players, the anxiety of the younger players, and the determination of the coaches. My coaching experiences were at two very small schools in Kentucky – Campbellsville High School and the now defunct Mt. Sterling High School. Both had enrollments of approximately 350 students, and only 30-35 players would try out for the team.

We launched the year with "two-a-day" sessions, the first at 8:00am, and then again at 4:00pm. Due to the heat, the first week of practice would be in shorts and helmets with no contact, just lots of running and conditioning.

By the end of the first week, only the true football players with honest desire and talent would remain, and the intense focus was getting down to the basics of the game. The coaches divided the team into four groups for individual learning sessions: the linemen, offensive backs, ends and linebackers, and the defensive backs. Coaches assigned to each group would fine tune the skills of the individual players in order for them to play their respective positions.

After mastering the drills, the groups were merged in order to learn the offense and defense. This lasted several days before the actual scrimmages began. Many of my former players have told me that this was the part of August that they found the most fun and memorable. It is worth noting that, due to injuries or the loss of players, we occasionally had to practice with half-line scrimmages because we could not dress 22 players at the same time.

Each of these schools had traditions that had been established over many years of success. For that reason, we were able to compete effectively against schools with larger enrollments and greater numbers of players on their teams.

A good example is Mt. Sterling High School. We once defeated a Lexington school (Henry Clay) which had more than 100 players – while we had a mere 33 players dressed to play. At the beginning of that game, the opposing coach had his team members come out of the dressing room running in single file run through the goal posts in order to intimidate our team. When lined up on the side line, they looked like an army. But MSHS wasn't about to roll over for them. We won with a score of 8-0. Because of heart and tradition, our players believed they could beat any team they faced. They proved themselves true to the task many times.

My most outstanding memory of coaching came during the 1969 season at Mt. Sterling. The Trojans had 38 players who made the team. We may have lost the first game when we played Tompkinsville in the long-established Recreation Bowl, but we only lost one other game that entire season. Never before had I witnessed such desire and performance from such a small group of die-hard football players. We entered the State Playoffs with a record of 8-2-1, with a Class A *Courier-Journal* ranking of number 4 in the state.

The first Playoff game was against Dayton on Jones Field in Mt. Sterling. Our team got to use the new field house for first time at that game. The date was November 17, 1969, and this was the third game for the Trojans in only three weeks. The first half was scoreless, but the Trojans scored first in the third quarter when Eddie Miller hit Charlie Bill Owens for a 34-yard pass. We prevailed with a final score was 24-0, and the Trojans moved on to the second round.

On Friday, November 21, 1969, Mt. Sterling met the defending State Champions from Lynch in Harlan County. The temperature was bitterly cold, and fires were burning in large barrels on each side of the playing field. The Trojans scored first on a Miller-to-Robert Brooks pass in the first quarter, and Owens then ran the ball for a two-point conversion. The half ended with a score of 8-0. In the third quarter, Lynch scored and added two points for an 8-8 tie.

During the fourth quarter, Lynch scored again to make the score

14-8, and their home town fans went crazy. With time running out, Coach Ishmael called a time-out and sent in a special play. Miller again passed the ball, but this time it was to Doug Cunningham in the end zone for the touchdown with only 46 seconds left to play. The game was tied 14-14. Ishmael decided to run the ball, and Charlie Bill succeeded by literally dragging two Lynch players into the end zone. The score was now 16-14. In the final few seconds of the game, Owens intercepted a pass and held on to run out the clock. The climax of that season came on Thanksgiving Day at UK's Stoll Field when we defeated Bardstown 20-12 to capture the Class A State Championship. The Trojans scored first on a 20-yard pass to George Calico (who happens to now be my brother-in-law).

One of the most often discussed plays of the game came when Coach Ishmael called a tackle-eligible pass play. Tackle Perry Colliver lined up as the last man on the left side of the field, making him eligible to receive a pass. Miller passed to Coliver on the one yard line and Colliver made his way into the end zone. Later, it was noted that this was the only time in the season that we had used this special play.

That season established a bond among those young men and their coaches which continues until this day, more than 40 years later. This is the best example that I know of the saying, "It is not the size of the dog in the fight, but the size of the fight in the dog!"
I still admire those guys for their heart and undeniable will to win. I remain proud of each of them and of my association with that team. And just as surely as August rolls around every year, I will continue to recall those players with great affection and that season with tremendous pride. There remains a bond between me and those boys that truly is worth more than gold.

Author's Note: In the summer of 2012, I was visiting with one of my former football players, Omar Prewitt, in front of his business in Mt. Sterling. As we reminisced about our football past, another player, Tony Fritts, joined us. Before long, Al Blevins and Mac McCormick arrived on the scene. The five of us talked about Mt. Sterling High School football for quite some time while standing right there on the street. It was if we had just finished practice and were going home to play again another day.

On my way home, I stopped in Camargo and visited with another Trojan quarterback, my friend Tom Orme. The memories are priceless.

Me in my classroom

'Silver in the Mine'

Upon gathering some information for an article about Powell County teachers who had achieved the status of National Board Certification, I was met with the question, "How long did you teach chemistry?" My answer, as always, brought a shocked look to the one asking the question. "Thirty-eight years," I replied.

Each time I reiterate the 38 years, I myself am amazed that I was able to last that long in the classroom. I suppose one reason was that I started at the young age of 20.

When I graduated from Mt. Vernon High School on a Friday night in May of 1962, my automobile was packed to make the trip to the University of Kentucky on the following Monday. I received my degree in 1965 and began my teaching career in the middle of that year.

Even as a freshman at UK, my decision had been established concerning my chosen profession – to teach high school science. While a student at Mt. Vernon High School, two of my instructors made such a strong impact on me that I wanted to be just like them. Those teachers were Dorothy Landrum, who taught Biology, and Charles "Tuck" Baker, who taught Chemistry. Because of them, my mind was made up – a teacher I would be.

In the first freshman biology class that I taught at Campbellsville High School, there was a young man, whom I will refer to as "Roger," who sat near the back of the room. Roger did not make eye contact with me, nor did he ask any questions concerning my lessons. It was evident that he was not as popular as many of the privileged children in the class. As the class progressed, he continued to be extremely quiet and reserved.

As time passed, Roger appeared bored and uninterested in the subject of biology. I was determined to learn about his disinterest in my class. One day, I decided to use my planning period to visit with the school's guidance counselor. I wanted to find out how Roger was performing in his other classes. Much to my dismay, he was having difficulty in several of his classes – even though he had tested quite well.

The next day, I asked him to remain after class, hoping we could make a connection. His first comment was, "I don't have all of my textbooks." Without asking why, I simply walked to my desk and handed him my copy of *Modern Biology*. His eyes opened wide, and he exclaimed, "I can't take *your* book!"

"Sure you can," I replied. "Tomorrow I want you to be able to discuss with me and the rest of the class the assignment that I gave you today." I told him to follow me to the bookstore, and I gave him the rest of his textbooks. He looked at me with gratitude in his sad eyes. He finally said, "Thank you so much, Mr. Griffin. You will not be disappointed in me."

Benjamin Franklin once said, "Genius without education is like *silver in the mine.*" Because of Roger's academic scores, I just knew he was capable. I was determined for him be part of the class discussions.

The next day, he raised his hand in response to every question that I asked! I called on him several times, and the rest of the class watched in disbelief. His answers were both accurate and quite profound.

At the end of class that day, Roger approached my desk and said, "I love this class, Mr. Griffin, and you will not be disappointed in me again." And I never was. When it came time for grades to be posted, Roger had the highest average in my biology class.

The following year, he took my chemistry class and again achieved the highest grade. When he graduated, he was awarded the honor of Salutatorian. On that day, with tears flowing down his cheeks, he hugged me and said, "You are my favorite teacher, Mr. Griffin." Those remarks made me feel like Dorothy Landrum and

"Tuck" Baker rolled into one. Do you now understand why I taught for 38 years?

I recently learned that Roger has earned his doctorate and is now teaching science at a major western university.

"Much I have learned from my teachers, more from my colleagues, but most from my students." (The Talmud)

I was proud to be a life-long member of the teaching profession. (My dear mother taught school for many years herself, and my brother also taught for a while.) Someone once said, "Teaching is the essential profession, the one that makes all other professions possible."

It is time we give teachers our undivided support and encouragement. Most of them enter the profession to help shape future generations. Untapped potential is always *silver in the mine*!